I0734318

What We Love

Aster(ix) Journal

presents

What We Love

Fall 2016

⁎⁎⁎

Edited by
Angie Cruz,
Madhu H. Kaza, and M.L. Vargas

BLUE SKETCH PRESS | PITTSBURGH

See page 174 for individual copyright information.

Published via Blue Sketch Press, Pittsburgh.
www.bluesketchpress.com

What We Love: An Aster(ix) Anthology / Aster(ix) Journal
Edited by Angie Cruz, Madhu H. Kaza, & M.L. Vargas— 1st ed.
ISBN (print) 978-1-942547-04-4 (trade paperback)
1-942547-04-8 (ISBN-10)

Cover Design by Little Owl Creative, www.littleowlcreative.com
Cover Image by Rachel Eliza Griffiths www.rachelelizagriffiths.com/
Copy-Edited by Joseph N. Welch, III.

First Edition: November 2016

Printed in the United States of America
9 8 7 6 5 4 3 2 1

This issue would not have been possible without the following contributing editors:

Amy Sara Carroll
Arielle Greenberg
Yona Harvey
Idra Novey
Emily Raboteau
Zohra Saed
Purvi Shah
Sun Yung Shin

Aster(ix) Journal

Aster(ix) is usually published 2-3 times a year in print with additional content online.

Funded in part by the Dietrich School of Arts and Sciences and the Department of English at University of Pittsburgh.

Contents

What We Love

A conversation between Angie Cruz, Madhu Kaza and Marta Lucia Vargas

Madhu H. Kaza: When I think of the idea behind "What We Love" I think back to an exhibition that the conceptual artist Fred Wilson curated several years ago for a gallery in New York. The show didn't have a theme—the theme was basically: Art that Fred Wilson Likes and Wants to Include in His Show. I loved that gesture. Particularly because—if you know Fred Wilson's work—he is such an incisive thinker about art history, race, and the way that our gaze is shaped by institutions and power. So this was not a scenario in which a white male curator was making the usual move of promoting his personal (or market calculated) taste as the universal standard of greatness. It was far more interesting. It was transparently subjective. I read it as an assertion of freedom, a way of claiming more space for black subjectivity.*

Women and people of color are often boxed in by publishers and cultural institutions—there are a limited number of things that we are supposed to talk about or like or want. An acquaintance of mine, an African American college professor, remarked that her colleagues listen very closely when she talks about race, but they are uninterested in what she might say about gardening or architecture or grandchildren. I want to hear what she thinks about any of these things, whatever is important to her.

"What We Love" was conceived so that we could publish whatever work excited us. I think a basic impulse in editing this issue for me also had to do with bringing a kind of honesty, a baring of our values and aesthetic attitudes to the work. The issue has its own omissions, contradictions, and blind-spots. But I think it's an exciting place to start. I'd also been thinking of Odysseas Elytis' poem, "Sun the First," from a section of *Eros, Eros, Eros* called "What I Love," which I recall reading to both of you when we were re-imagining Aster(ix) and dreaming up what this issue could be. The poem includes the lines, "What I love is always being born/ What I love is beginning always." This is also the first issue produced with our new group of contributing editors. So here we are beginning again with "What We Love."

Angie Cruz: Those lines in particular alight an aspect of editing Aster(ix), true since its inception, of always beginning again. The journal has had so many rebirths, incarnations. The constant shape shifting of the journal exposes how I personally have been working through and against imagined constraints. I've been practicing how to intentionally occupy this potentially liberatory literary space, being more courageous and free, as writers, readers, lovers of things. When we looked through the varied works solicited to us by our expanded community of contributing editors I had to continually ask myself, do I love this? Is it a beautiful work? All of this is subjective, but why isn't my subjectivity as valid as everyone else's? And what do I mean by love? *In The Fire Next Time*, Baldwin describes it this way: "Love takes off the masks that we fear we cannot live without and know we cannot live within. I use the word "love" here not merely in the personal sense but as a state of being, or a state of grace—not in the infantile American sense of being made happy but in the tough and universal sense of quest and daring and growth." So when reading the works for this issue, I tried to keep asking myself, what's fresh about this piece, am I moved, puzzled, is it daring?

ML Vargas: If you both remember, a revamping of Aster(ix) came about over a dinner in November, 2015, where we shared our excitement about journals, books and our place among the conversations with which we felt most aligned, most challenged.

The print issue of "What We Love" naturally arose from enacting that original conversation, by bringing more voices to the table, where we are creating a home with good bones and impeccable intentions, so we can share writing that moves us. We revisited and have revised the Aster(ix) vision to embrace the known and unknown; the courageous and the unpredictable; the real and the unreal; to wrestle with the possible and the impossible; jaguar's chesty roar; magic; what's censored and omitted; love and devotion. What has come forth, through conversations and connections,reading, rereading and arguing over submissions in Madhu's bed/oir, was directed by what we love, with love as the torch bearer.

AC: And this has produced an issue that to me reflects an unapologetic freedom. The works are varied, maybe even all over the place in style, themes, but they all inhabit a "sprezzatura of an infant" as described by Agamben in *Nudities*, where he says " the ways in which we do not know things are just as important (and perhaps even more important) as the way we know them….an unselfconsciouness." Beauty and enchantment lies in that space.

When we made the call for this issue, "What We Love," the editors solicited writers they loved and then we looked at the work and asked ourselves if it was work we loved. And the fun for me was in the ways we disagreed and agreed. All of us are wildly different from each other and look for different things in our reading. But we discovered how we're most interested in ensuring that Aster(ix) nurtures and prioritizes works that surprise us and are doing something novel. Dia Felix's story is a good example of this. And perhaps that is why we chose to start the issue with it. It embodies, like many of the chosen works, the energy, play and seriousness, the wild splat.

MHK: "What We Love" brings together the work of twenty one amazing writers. I'm happy that we were able to include writers who are not based in the U.S.: Vahni Capildeo, Saudamini Deo, Magda Kapa, and Marie NDiaye. I love that there are odd, unlikely resonances between the works. For instance, green haunts the women in Marie NDiaye's Self-Portrait in Green. Vahni Capildeo's piece ends with the lines, "Yesterday I walked again in the green space./ This has been thought for you." Capildeo's work is dense and beautiful in its own right, but these lines lingered in my mind differently in connection with NDiaye's work. And I read NDiaye's work in conversation with Miranda Mellis' excerpt from The Spokes. Both pieces explore difficult relationships between women through otherworldly encounters and both are gorgeously written.

I also appreciate how different many of the works in the issue are. We did not work from one idea or voice or aesthetic viewpoint. Apart from the three of us, there were a number of other editors who contributed to this issue—I would like to acknowledge Arielle Greenberg, Yona Harvey, Idra Novey, Emily Raboteau, Zohra Saed, Purvi Shah, and Sun Yung Shin. This issue contains work that they sent our way, and so it really is a collective statement of what we love.

I want to mention, too, a piece that is not in this issue but which was important to our thinking when we began working together to re-launch Aster(ix) with a new collective of editors and contributing editors. Jenelle Troxell wrote a piece for Aster(ix) online about Margaret Anderson and Jane Heap. Anderson and Heap were founders of The Little Review, an early 20th century journal that published modernist, feminist, surrealist, queer, anarchist writers. We're not modernist white women—I think we and our aesthetics are more all over the place—but the spirit of their work informed our process.

AC: Admittedly, working with Jenelle on her short piece highlighted why we should continue publishing creative criticism and also contextualized the work we have been doing for so many years. I was quite seduced by the history of little magazines. So many of the important ones (not surprisingly) were started by women and at their own expense and sacrifice. But aside from the sacrifices of both time and money that it takes to keep these efforts going, what I loved about Heap and Anderson was the boudoir description. In Heap's meeting room, editors and contributors would gather on a swinging bed in the middle of the room because editing is an intimate act. And when looking for work they stressed how they didn't want to be bored. Boredom was their litmus and that felt quite liberatory to me. Why can't we choose work that does not bore us? Us meaning women of color. Us meaning politicized women of color and our allies. How can we recreate a space where we can also "fight" and work through what is beauty, what is important, what works should earn a space in this journal we are nurturing?

MLV: In thinking about the future of Aster(ix), I'd also like to swing back to the past. Thanks to Jenelle, we can celebrate this moment as 100 years after Jane Heap and Margaret Anderson. While we are addressing the public possibilities, we are also deeply interested in the "life inspired." What is the criteria of the wild imagination for us? I am guided by Heap and Anderson's "libidinal charge" and Audre Lorde's "erotic`electrical charge" and always, Frederico García Lorca's duende. Being held by such forces allows us to ask, in Clarice Lispector's words, what would one say in the "madness of sincerity" and in the "madness of free invention?" How does this wild dream? What is its form? Who vows to participate in its revelation?

As Gloria Anzaldua's daughters we court the wound, the edges, where we find possible and impossible exchanges. I very much love how Aisha Durham, an Aster(ix) contributor, defined both a challenge and an inspiration: "I live on the margins of my discipline." The September 1916 issue of the Little Review left thirteen pages blank as a space for the missing content in response to a call for creative criticism. The thirteen blank pages in this issue are my invitation for wild imaginative im/possibilities, play, both on the page and in the life, wherever the blurrings of the private and the public create new encounters, new galaxies. This blurring fueled by love, is our transformative future.

* Though I recall the exhibition described here, I can't find any documentation of it. So there is a small chance that somehow I transposed events and made up this story. That would not negate its essential truth.

Alex, Please, Delight Us

Dia Felix

Dolores County got a new public high school. It aggregated the three existing schools into one and it was supposed to be the future. It smelled like a luxury boutique and radiated light from its white tiles to invigorate and focus the students. The school bells were recordings of Tibetan prayer bells, or was that a real bell? There were grass roofs and solar panels and a track for running made from recycled car tires. In the staff break room, a proper chrome espresso machine gleamed and whirred. The hippest coffee company in town had given it to the school as a gift, and offered to provide staff with fair trade coffee for the first year. On the first day, the students—about 2200 had enrolled—were quiet and bewildered, like ants who had lost their way.

Soon enough though the kids were acting like kids. Liver-colored globs of gnawed-up gum appeared in the elegant native plant garden. The born again Christian kids gathered before school to pray around the flagpole, holding hands. Torment was dispatched from the jocks to Marsha the custodian, who had an uncommonly long forehead and slow-motion way of ambulating, but Nefertiti cheekbones and a dramatic, stunning shape in the back. The colorful and confident basketball girls claimed their bench, ate Doritos. The one French girl sat under a tree and ate raspberries alone. The drama clubbers found each other, a quiver of pale arms. There was even a reputed coven of witches—among the shaggy rockers and trim goths who glowered out from beside the elevator. They liked to draw each other in charcoal during lunch. There were rumors about them—that they sucked each others blood, that three of them were like, in a relationship, and that they were going to do something freaky at Homecoming to protest something? Animal rights?

One of the reputed witches, Alex, is looking at you, with cutoff black shorts, lacy black tights, tall combat boots, and a large black sweater, a fat loose knit, faded from washing. She pulls it over her wrists, tangling her hands in her sleeves. She doesn't want to sit down. Black and green eye makeup under her oversized glasses, pale skin studded with a smattering of abused blemishes, dyed black hair in a style you don't understand, is it an accident or is it meant to look like that, tight with lumps, then a little tiny bun like a chopped tail.

You're in you're new office, with a shiny wood floor repurposed from an old bowling alley. You have a large window which looks out on a crisply blacked ocean of parking lot.

You say: *If there is going to be an intervention at the Homecoming Dance, you must tell us now, Alex.*

Alex, who has already told you that she is going to "practice strategic silence" says...nothing. Her hands gnaw at her hands.

I am asking you if you are planning to do something which disrupts sanctioned school activities.

Well, I'm a witch, she says.

And then she gets up and leaves, so quiet, like an eel.

Later, Alex is sitting in her AP Art History class, the lights are off and they're looking at slides of naked women—colorful, wild, fauve, tropical. Giant white flowers, smooth brown skin. It's warm and dark and sticky.

Alex, will you illuminate us? the teacher, Ms. Arndt, asks.

Alex rises, turns the lights on. Everyone remains asleep, some with their heads on the desk, others in a normal seated position but with gently closed eyes. It's a small class, maybe 15 kids. No one moves. Alex and Ms. Arndt look at each other, they smile together. What a weird thing.

Well? Says Ms. Arndt, in a stage whisper. *Should we turn the lights back off? Seems like everyone else needs to rest.*

Alex clicks the lights back off. For a moment she feels like she is just as much the teacher as the teacher is. Why not? A sharp snap of glee in her belly.

I guess I'll go get some coffee from the teachers lounge? says Ms. Arndt. *Do you want anything?*

I'd love an espresso, says Alex.

Alex and Ms. Arndt sip coffee and chat just outside the classroom, on a bench in the pleasant shade. Alex looks at her teacher's bones, the clean jaw and the clavicle or whatever you call the one that shoots from shoulder to shoulder in the front, it's very refined.

The bell sweetly dings, the American teens lift and amble dazedly out of the classroom, many of them in bright sweatshirts. They passively enjoy the teenage army drifting by.

Wanna smoke a J? asks Ms. Arndt, in a true whisper.

Sure, giggles Alex. No one she knows says "a J." Maybe that's what they said in the eighties?

Let's get outta here, says Ms. Arndt.

In Ms. Arndt's silver Toyota Tercel now, wow. She drives to Sweetie's Grove, but that feels weird because it's such a teen hangout, so they immediately turn around and drive to the Sports Arena parking lot, which feels more like a general criminal hangout.

The bagel shop is closing. The hot girl who wears tank tops is struggling to carry a large black trash bag to the dumpster, her blonde ponytail swinging tensely.

Then she goes back into the store. Suddenly Alex overwhelmingly craves a toasted bagel with sweet raisin walnut cream cheese. Ms. Arndt swings into the parking lot. Strawberry is what they have left. *We're actually closed*, clarifies the hot girl. *But I'll make it for you if you want it.* Alex wants it.

Alex and Ms. Arndt split the bagel. The taste is amplified, the smell immense.

I wanted to ask the class, said Ms. Arndt, swallowing, *why do you think teeth are so rarely depicted in paintings? And why, when they do appear, do they read as so menacing?*

Also, compare and contrast the Venus of Willendorf with what you believe are the 'Venus' figures of our time. Discuss body ideals and how you imagine they are formed. Do not worry about substantiating everything. Really just reflect like you would with a friend. Do the best you can to be honest.

Ms. Arndt is so beautiful right now and those are beautiful questions. Alex wants to tell her this, but says something about "je ne sais quoi" and that phrase is suddenly the funniest and most ridiculous thing either of them has ever heard or spoken. Alex is practically gagging up the pink cream cheese she's laughing so hard. What a dumb thing to say, *you are so beautiful, you have this certain....Oh, I don't know. Nevermind.*

Next day in AP Art History class, Alex arrives, glides in, naked. Naked, no clothes, no shoes. Her body is as smooth as a fresh lightbulb right out of the box. Ms. Arndt doesn't mind that Alex is naked when Alex glides into class, naked. Ms. Arndt is bowled over, actually. The lights are on and everyone is staring at Alex's nude body naked nude.

Alex, will you please de-light us? asks Ms. Arndt.

Alex, naked, shuts off the lights, and with a bit of rustling and rearranging, the class turns their focus to the screen, where there's a painting by Cezanne, a sea of cubey roofs which invite the future of painting. Alex settles into a cool plastic chair—which feels weird and tickly against her exposed intimate parts, but soon feels fine actually—

and pays close attention.

The Homecoming dance came and went and was free of any sort of intervention, allowing those students with conventional tastes to enjoy themselves without mockery. Alex was not disciplined for being naked at school, and did not do it again.

Three Poems

Khadijah Queen

I never met Bill Cosby but I met Beverly Johnson at Magic Mountain with my dad & my sister one summer in the mid-1980s & she had on an oversized cardigan & jeans casual but lovely my dad chatted her up while we rode the Colossus with her daughter he said he asked for her number & she politely declined I remember her grace & regality & lace-up boots she sat on the bench with her feet crossed at the ankle so when she went public about Cosby drugging & trying to assault her I immediately believed her & not him I have seen enough of powerful men by now to know she had nothing to gain by getting in the fray & the truth of beauty means both spotlights & shadows find you & it takes more than instinct to know where to stand on the stage & I don't mean looks all the time I mean all women are all beautiful & I wish we knew it in ways that make us realize the relative insignificance of the arrangement of external features so we might as well have a little fun with it & not get so caught up & my dad had a lot of nerve right I mean men have a lot of fucking nerve in general & I think my sister & I had on matching Hawaiian shirts that day & wore them tucked in I didn't wear that shirt again & not long after that I fell in love with fashion & asked my dad to start buying me issues of Vogue

We met Shai at the Fox Hills Mall I remember because we were trying on clothes & trying to convince one of our friends not to shoplift a lace push-up bra & panty set she had a date that night with her crush & no cute underwear we said Girl you better keep your clothes on & who walked in the store but the tall cute one with the curly hair she forgot all about her date & her draws because she looooooved Shai especially the tall cute one with the curly hair she got dressed & got a hug & an autograph I probably had on one of my dad's old BOSS sweatshirts that shrank in the dryer because I didn't have many clothes I was 16 & that was the year our house burned down & I left Beverly Hills High where my fashion technology teacher presented Gone With the Wind as a good example of costume design so I requested to be excused to the library where I read The Autobiography of Malcolm X until the class finished watching all 238 minutes of that BS

I met Keyshawn Johnson on the USC campus in one of the dorm rec rooms it was low lit & he was playing pool the friend I was with pointed him out & he nodded at us & shook hands I had on a green denim knee-length Fubu jacket & black bodysuit with my sister's dark green men's Levi's for the low rise waist before they made those for women & fake black Timbs I don't remember why I was there but wherever my friend invited me I always tried to go we were just hanging out probably he was in his second or third year at SC & I think that was the night he felt me up & I did like & want him but not like that I wanted something more like love we had known each other since middle school but didn't talk for a while after that although eventually we did become friends again & so much happened between us I could write a book about it but I've lost interest in pain

Untitled & Ze

Amy Sara Carroll

S**************:**
T************L**
ARS IN A BOW
El Paso.

Ze

All summer we set out to make an undocumentary. Rosa Alcalá taught me the word. I introduced myself to her because I love *Undocumentaries*. Our email messages were brief to one another. Mine were all fanfare, hers, gracious. Shyly in one of my messages I admitted that three years earlier Ricardo, Zé, and I had driven from Corpus Christi to San Diego. Stopping in El Paso, I'd wanted to invite her to have coffee with us. I'd wanted to call her out of the blue—something I never feel or do—without an introduction. Instead, because the night was dark and twinkling, I'd written a concave poem, "Stars in a bowl: El Paso." The next morning we walked into Ciudad Juárez. It was 2010. We went to a Sunday market that Ricardo had known as a child. Ricardo bought me a necklace of saints. I stumbled with Zé in the street. A nearby pedestrian helped me to my feet, blessed me, and told me to go home. That was six years ago when the Federal Police occupied the city, when the front page of its leading newspaper queried, "¿Qué quieren de nosotros?" This summer is haunted, but indifferent to rememory, as expanded cinema. I want to tell Rosa Alcalá that we filmed a "poet tree." Hanging from its branches were words like leaves. Fairy houses dotted its roots. Dulce and Zé built environments, dug holes and ditches, sculpted sundials so we'd always be able to tell time what we really think: it was the hour of my defeat but also hours of all things good and sweet, ungendered as our "No Movie" or Zé without his accent.

St. George's Bell

Magda Kapa

St. George's bell was gone.

The cleaning woman, an Albanian who had been living in the village for almost eighteen years, one of the first to cross the border in search for work, coming all the way down to the Peloponnese, mostly on foot and occasionally hitch-hiking, noticed it first. She went to clean up and prepare the chapel for the annual liturgy on St. George's name day, April 23rd.

The priest, terribly shocked at the news, ran immediately to the cafenion where the village men were enjoying their first coffee in the open. (Spring was really here now and even a Greek winter can cause depressions.)

St. George's bell had been ringing since 1907, and it was the village students' present to the newly built chapel, financed mainly by their collection of donations. It was from a time when students wore uniforms and caps and needed almost half a day to arrive at the village by horse carriage from Athens, nowadays just a one and a half hour drive away.

During the German occupation, St. George's bell rang to warn the partisans whenever the German soldiers mobilized towards the hills where the partisans were hiding and from where the chapel watched over the village. The men now in the cafenion were the sons and grandsons of those men sent running scared up the hills when the bell spoke to them.

A spontaneous meeting was held in the cafenion. A few phone calls and a few more of the village elders joined the angry round. It didn't take long and, as always happens on these occasions, the foreigners were blamed. The Albanians had been the usual suspects for years and years. But they were not illegals anymore, didn't sleep under the orange trees in improvised tents, didn't have to steal everything not nailed down and sell it in order to survive till the next job appeared. No, the Albanians now had labor permits and lived in houses, their kids went to school here and were actually the reason, a few years ago, why the village elementary school was not closed down. The village birth rate had dipped too low. Blame it on the stress of modern times.

Spirits were already somehow calmed. The new illegals, the young Africans who usually hung around in the main district town, were soon also disqualified as bell thieves. The local teenagers explained that they were too well controlled by their own Mafia, which was not interested in bells but in whores and pirated CDs and DVDs. They knew this of course, because they were grateful customers themselves.

There was just one possibility left: the Gypsies (no one called them Romani here, not even they themselves).

Yes, the Gypsies controlled the scrap metal market and since the prices of copper and iron skyrocketed, the Gypsies had ransacked, bought, taken, or dismantled anything they could. Two neighbors went to court last month, accusing each other of selling the iron posts that had marked the shared border of their properties, before discovering that the posts had been stolen, like everybody else's in the area.

The metal prices shot up after the real estate crisis in the U.S. for reasons that no one in this cafenion could really explain; it's just the way capitalism works.

The villagers agreed that St. George's bell, which had been ringing for this village ever since 1907 likely landed in capitalism's melting pot, together with the iron posts marking land ownership. And not only the communists in the cafenion laughed at this joke.

It was agreed that a new bell would be ordered at the best bell foundry in the prefecture. Who knows, something from the old bell might find its way into the new one. It seems our world is quite small.

Haricots Verts

Leila Christine Nadir

Sometimes two seagulls land on a chimney on a blue-sky morning. Sometimes one flies away and the other seagull stays, perching there for nearly an hour, like it's got nowhere to be but right there, talons gripping red brick. Sometimes this happens atop the building across from where you sit, eating a bowl of oatmeal, on the second-story balcony of your room at the Lord Camden Inn, on the coast of Maine. Sometimes, as you chew (slowly, because you've read this improves digestion), another seagull flies over and lands below the chimney this time, on the rooftop, so there are two again. They stare in the northwestern direction, toward the bay of sailboats, and you think of Richard Russo because the Camden Deli across the street claims he wrote *Empire Falls* there (it's emblazoned on a wooden plaque), and you realize from this claim and from the cold cuts on the menu that Richard does not care much for fresh vegetarian food like you. Sometimes one seagull crouches down low on the chimney, as if it's tucking itself in for a before-noon nap, and it stays this way for a while, as you eat the last blueberries from your bowl, until it stands up, stretches its head into the air, and lets out a squawk. And you don't know why but when you see this you think of the Italian pizza you had with your boyfriend, on your first night in Paris, ten years ago, at a table next to two American college students dressed in J.Crew on an awkward date. And then you remember how some weeks later you carried a bag of dirty clothes down Rue Férou, to a laundromat a few blocks from the fountain at St. Sulpice. It was a breezy day in July, perfect weather for drying laundry in the sun, but you dropped coins into the dryer because last time you hung wet tank-tops and skirts from your apartment windows, Madame Barrere, your old landlady, knocked on your door and pointed a skinny finger. While the clothes tossed in the machine, you stepped into a bistro for a snack and tried to order in French but couldn't remember whether to pronounce the "h" in *haricots verts*. And then one Camden seagull flies away and the other stays put and then another seagull arrives. And you wish every day could start this way but perhaps it's okay they do not.

From *The Olga Poems*

Laura Sims

Olga-Helga, I value

your stuff. With my odalisque
curves, my delirious
cockatiel heart

Be aware: I'm unusual. Oh

I'm the stuffer
who'll stuff you
to gills
with (my) gold

You bagged

me good without
soiling your prawns, Olga-
Helga. I drift
through the aqueous blue. Toodle-
loo, toodle-loo. You
bagged me, I bit you.
You brained me, I made you
a chainsaw for felling
trees. Isn't love? Such a
lowly condition. I'm a
great big
banana
for you, and you
you're my
wide-brimmed
yellow-clad
fool

I've done my time in the hippodrome, working

shit out. I'm the blonde
with blue eyes, I'm Dick,
the dining room furniture
king, I'm a sad ol' dissolute
seraphim. Olga, come
hither and do
what agrarian villagers
do. I keep
my hands whiter
than napkins, myself. I'm
the brain,
and a basketcase, baby. Don't shy away—
even you
can come
closer, come
write to me
on my
Electronic
Box.

I've been kinda bored

I've been taking
a bunch
of hot/funny photos. Should I
post them
all over
your rubbery breasts? That's
not talk from a "dying world"
Olga—that's straight
from the cradle of
life/sex/death. Here I am
banked on the river,
braiding
my hair. Where are you
little silver-scaled
bird, immaterial
queen?
Face-down
and shivering
in
the
abyss

eating words

Olga, you linger

and cling
to the hive, to that
dirty unworthy metropolis.
Girl, you go
strutting around.
Like a slattern. Doggy.
Effete. The world
brings plague
to its smuttiest squirrels while you
nosh
down at Wing Stop. Take a
fetuslike look
into space; now sit
with the blood
and the triumph
of brain. Abide

in that place. Down the yellowbrick road
we were Pilates and
trilobites

once we were wholly
divine

Olga Olga Olga your Zoloft is mine

I love you
like Emma. I love you like
Pride. I love you like Jane Austen
dollars, I love
to insert you in snide
conversations with fuckwads
-slash-
colleagues of mine. Alas
we are not
metatarsal, we bones
we belong
in the hands. Muscled shut
you're shinola-won't-
grease-you-back-
into-my-life. Mrs. Darling
my privy
you're privy
to all whom the jillions
despise

Lo in the water, Olga,

you hold me. How long is your chain and how barbed
your panoptic maw

am I heavy to bear & contain am I human or

something that ruts. Rusts. And disintegrates. Now
I'm a merman coming
apart. Now a poisonous

cloud of red dust. I was exhaled
into the ducts
and then
and then

I blew up

Olga, who dresses

your hair, and who plucked
that purple-black
plumage you wear
from the ether? Not I—
I'm a decorous

turd. A dusted-down
armored-up suit
of conditions. As in: if you
have saturnine grace

if you've been false
or estranged

if you've arranged a bamboozle: I'll swaddle you

in my wet clinging metal. It's gentle.
Filigree. Silvery. Still
it's a chain

Olga, your kung pao

chicken is here. To lay
waste to your bowels. Grab
a glacier! Embrace it! Its surface
aglitter
with shit from the birds
of the centuries. Drink
the deep blue. Find it
cooling, steady. Let it
irrigate all
your canals, let it
sluice
you
out
until only bare rock
and your ironclad
gluttony
thrive

I Don't Yet Know if I Will Return

Saudamini Deo

Rahman suddenly took the pen from my hands and wrote in swirling ink: Qustuntuniya. In the 5th century, outside a small church, under a slightly furry skin, I remember chewing leaves while listening to the divine liturgy of St. John Chrysostom: I'd never heard anything like that before, and the world that had seemed nothing but a complete, locked mystery took on an evanescent quality. There was something more, something invisible following all of us. Was this sound then the manifestation of everything unknown, everything I had never understood before? Centuries earlier, the Indians called it Samaveda: song knowledge.

It was under the spell of this divine music that I'd made the fatal decision to be a human in my next life.

It is the last sentence of the liturgy that has influenced me: "Let us be attentive." Since hearing these words of incredible wisdom, I travel the surface of the earth by opening all of my senses: sight, hearing, touch, taste… Do I forget one? Perhaps the most valuable...

Another phrase says, "Peace to you who read." And I read and I read. From book to book, from poem to poem, my body became a library. You, my love, come read in me, come see the world through me.

Qustuntuniya, Qustuntuniya, I lie trapped in the middle of your arabesques.

***

With a camera in my hand, I followed light and color in the old streets of Prague. I looked at an old shop, its jaded window covered with a map of India, colored red, and while looking at my own reflection in it, I noticed another woman standing a little apart from me, only her back visible, her hair covered with an ancient veil. She suddenly started walking away. I didn't dare to turn my head and look at her, scared that she might not be there. And so, I looked at her on glass, following her reflection from window to window on an endless street, her face still invisible, only her dark skin peering through sometimes between the sleeves and gloves. I thought I could follow her till the end of the world, till the edge of insanity and beyond.

I saw the end of endlessness. I saw.

Her face, a vertigo. She, the black Madonna.

***

In every dusty corner of this city both cursed and magical, I sought out the Golem. I was looking for this mischievous life, this being that no one has ever seen, now tucked away in the attic of a condemned ageless synagogue. Golem, what do you do with your days? Do you remember the lives that you, not even human, protected? Do you read anything? In what language? The ones before Babel? What do you think, in your prison of stone and paper? If I could, I'd read to you.

***

I promised never to return to Paris. To France. Too much or too little is spent there. The clash of colors, in Provence: lavender, mimosa, fragrances of Grasse, blue-green olive trees contrasting with the ocher of the earth, the shock of Matisse, the sea as blue as azure eyes.

Paris, populated ghost hearts absent or not yet identified. Paris, a scar that was still open, or that only wanted to open up. Like Karen Blixen, I could write: "I had a heart, in France." Was it bleeding?

I do not yet know if I will return.

A heart. A heart, my heart, in France.

I do not know if I will return. I will return. I do not know. I will return.

(Untitled #5, #1, #6)

Saretta Morgan

Running my dog through the park. Face twisted wet and unbearable, I turn to every passing stranger / the lake's frozen surface / a family of grace-jawed geese, I say *I don't deserve this.*

But (God blessed me) (some way I have been always-asking).

There are several shapes of this day. A backless gown. All the bars I held so that my arm bones wouldn't obscure views of my chest. A 900 ML canister of contrast material self-administered in 15-minute intervals over the course of 2 hours. The VA hospital is, more than anything, boring as fuck. Every now and then something incredible splits apart.

In December I broke up with my therapist. A white man. Jewish. Gay. Raised in the Bronx. The Bronx Bronx—not Riverdale. Several perspectives from which to conceive of oppression, nevertheless, not a clue what Black mental health might look like. To most of his questions, I answered neither, or both. Still, it was difficult to move on.

I have always been running. Running and asking. Asking by running. The world calls this in a woman: fickle. I call it terrifying and have only resisted burning down every means of escape because I know what happens to a Black woman without a place to—: no, because I know—

The Spokes (excerpt)

Miranda Mellis

When I set out on this trip, I planned to come back. It's true that when I embarked, the return date of my trip was not set, but I had not imagined this... duration. If that is what it is. I remember the high, winding, narrow roads along the coast, the vertigo

And I remember at the ferry building there were a series of warnings, one of which was about the peculiar sort of "jet lag" one sustains in a realm whose primary substance is not time. The customs agent had recited, and required me to repeat after her, line by line, a litany of warnings about the nature of my destination. The only thing I remember now is the first warning: *Do not eat the food*, which I did, of course, within the first "day" (though that unit of time becomes meaningless without the sun).

I picked up my bag and boots after running the security gauntlet. As I turned to put on my boots, I tripped on the lip of a plastic mat. A uniformed young woman wearing latex gloves caught me as I toppled forward, and steadied me. She gripped my arm longer than was strictly necessary. She looked at me intently, with clear gray eyes. "Be careful, ma'am," she said. "Watch your step. Do you have a copy of the ferry schedule?" I did not. She turned around and pulled a small folded schedule from a stack behind her. She pressed it into my hand and firmly advised me not to lose it.

I laced up my black boots on a long wooden bench. There were several musicians emerging together from the line and collecting their instruments. A musician next to me opened a case and examined his trumpet. He put his mouthpiece on and blew. Then he put his trumpet together and played a familiar tune, the Melodians' "It's My Delight": *I love you, I love you, I really do.*

I walked slowly, listening to him play as I made my way down a ramp, a long hallway, and a flight of stairs. I came to the dock, a wobbling ramp of looped planks, and boarded the great rusty ferry, which was splattered with bird shit and tied off with ropes. I found a seat on the deck where long benches faced the diminishing shore. I fell asleep in my seat as the boat wended its way across the black river, over which lay a gray tule fog.

I dreamed I was in a bathtub. I had left the faucets on and the room was flooding. My mother, Silver, came in and rebuked me. She threw green towels on the floor and sopped up the water. We'll have to take these to the laundry, she said, they'd never dry in here. The floor became an ocean, the bathtub our boat. We were cold. We wrapped the towels around ourselves. We rode the waves but the tub was sinking. My mother bailed out the water with her hands, her hair gathered and scooped back. I looked around for a rescue ship as we sank. Then I looked down and saw my station wagon loping down into the heavy water.

I woke cold, unable to see, hear, or sense anything, not even my own weight. I had kicked over my purse, and some of its contents were beneath the bench. I bent over to collect them. A few pieces of paper, including the ferry schedule, fluttered away. I stood to chase after them when I saw a light, and then many more lights. I observed the crowd as we approached the shore. They flickered into view like so many lanterns. Three dogs ran back and forth along the quay. When I stepped off the boat, one trotted over, licking my hand and wagging his tail. The other two raised their heads and smiled. A lone child in a tilted orange hat with a rooster feather debarked behind me. The dogs ignored the child and the child ignored the dogs. The child talked instead to her hands, or should I say with her hands, which she was using as two puppets.

I petted the dog, who grinned amiably. The other dogs walked slowly back to the wall. One stretched, seeming to bow in my direction; he circled several times and then lay down a little heavily, as if something weighed on him. He nosed around himself chaotically, his dirty mane sticking out. Catching my eye, he glanced down the quay suggestively. I followed his gaze, and with a little shock I made out my mother. She looked just as I had last seen her, the day of her fall from the high wire. She wore her tight faux-emerald-and-ruby-studded tunic over a sheer dark-blue bodysuit, long, sharp macaw feathers in her bound hair. Glitter sparkled on her purple opalescent lips, and her eyes— one eyelid silver, the other gold— glistened brightly. Her short cape and slippers were sequined. For so long it seemed as if the gap between us would only grow. Now suddenly we were three feet apart.

Silver greeted me in the typically polyphonic voice of the dead, like the eager, chaotic valence of a tuning orchestra. Like crying, and a drill, and a xylophone, a chorus of one. "You must be hungry?" she said. I was dizzy with joy and nervousness as I went toward her, but she was looking past me. Who was she talking to? I turned around to see, behind me, the child: a much younger version of myself. Now I remembered the hat . . . I'd worn it constantly for months after my first unhappy haircut. I'd had hair down to my waist. My mother took me to the yo-

yo man, a geometer who had good scissors. When he was finished, my hair was the same length all the way around, a yo-yo–like sphere.

Clearly my mother did not see me, though I was standing right in front of her. Instead she saw this other, younger me. I spoke, I gestured. Neither of them made me out. I looked around. Was I the only invisible one here? Everyone seemed to be enjoying his or her reunions. My mother caressed my younger self's face, squatting down to gather her child into her arms. They walked hand in hand down the platform to a kiosk. My mother bought my younger self a tin of cold green gelatin, which she ate hungrily. I followed them I knew not where, my mother in her Spokes Cirque Rêve costume, as colorful as a summer bird, and my younger self in the slyly cocked orange hat.

It was not the first time in my life that I was invisible in a public place, if one can say of the afterworld that it is public. (Perhaps there is nowhere more public.) As a child I learned to blend in with the other spectators. I did not perform, though I longed to; my parents had other hopes for me. But the person I had grown into was not someone my mother knew anything about; perhaps that was the reason she could not see me as I was, but only as I had been. Unlike some, she had not spent her afterlife keeping current, i.e., haunting. She never returned the calls I made to her in my sleep. She never responded to the letters I wrote her on desperate days. She had her own death to live. In life too, she'd never talked much. When she was not rehearsing or performing, she was distracted and melancholy. On stage she smiled fervently, as if to smile was to bless. Offstage she was secretive, closemouthed.

I gather some families talk about everything (though all individuals have their reservoirs of silence). I only knew Silver was the last performer in the Spokes line, grew up in the same caravan that her ancestors had traveled in, performed the same tricks in the same towns and villages, and knew, just as her foremothers had known, that she risked the void every time she entered the ring. My father, Leo, was twice her age and an epileptic. "If nature had taken her course, I would have gone first," he had said. But gravity is nature.

It started to thunder in the distance: A storm approached, but no rain fell. The trumpet player passed me, walking slowly, playing Peggy Scott's "Lover's Holiday": *Maybe we can slip away.* I greeted him but he looked right through me. He was the only passenger I recognized. With my first pang of worry, I turned and watched him walking away. I wondered if I should follow, if he was on his way to catch a ferry home. But if time is not the substance of this universe, I thought, how could we know when it was "time" to return? I felt as if I could stay a thousand years or twenty minutes and it would make no difference. In any case, I had lost the ferry schedule.

I glanced around the station as I followed my mother and my younger self. I told myself to pay close attention to the path we were on, so that I could find my way back. I had never felt so disoriented; no sun, no East. At the end of the street, at the first right turn that my mother, myself, and I took, there was, hanging above the door of a very different kind of station farther down, Philip Guston's *The Tormentors.* I paused to look at the volcanic tongues of red paint. I told myself, when you see that again, you'll know you're on your way back. "What's that place?" my younger self asked, pointing. "The Tormentors, that's their station," my mother said, "in the Sinister Quarter."

The people at that station were gray, black, and white. Other than the painting, nothing at that station had any color. Light, absorbed or reflected by a surface, normally fractures and becomes color. It was as if the painting had absorbed all the available light, with none left over for the people or the pocked, rusted station.

We passed another station, Lautrec's *At the Moulin Rouge*. Was this my mother's stop? There was the trumpeter, standing just outside with all of the other musicians who had been on the ferry with me. They played exuberantly and comfortably, like old friends. A small crowd gathered and danced, including my mother and my younger self. They were a closed circuit, from which I was excluded. Why this should be the case I did not know. Was my invisibility the result of something I had failed to do? I had yet to learn the laws of recognition here, which are not moral in the same way they are at home, where dreaming is neither a virtue nor a skill (as it has proved to be here).

The crowd was not held by the music. Apparently the dead were incapable of paying attention to anything for very long. A few wandered toward a station with a fogged-in Malevich hanging overhead.

My mother and younger self sat on a bench and watched the dead mill around. I stood behind them and listened in on their conversation. "Where are they all going?" my younger self asked my mother. "Nowhere," said my mother. "But they look so busy, like they are going somewhere," my younger self said. "Well," Mother said, "they feel they should be." "But where are they supposed to be?" my younger self asked. "Nowhere in particular," Mother replied. "Why don't we tell them?" my younger self said. "You can try," my mother said. My younger self called out to the crowd, "Hey! Stop! Where are you going? You're dead — there's nowhere to go! Hey!" One shade stopped and asked, "Yes?" My younger self said, "Where are you going?" "I can't remember, but I must go on," he said. "Why do you think you have to go on?" she asked. But he was gone.

Where do I think I'm going? I said aloud. But of course, they weren't aware of me. I walked around to the bench where my mother and younger self were talking. I stretched out next to them and fell asleep. For the second time on this trip, I dreamed. In the dream there was a giant baby with a head like a white stone, big dark eyes like galaxies, and smooth infant skin. She stood slowly on her toddling legs, her arms outstretched, and when she stepped forward she caused an earthquake. The dream state we were in shook apart from the mainland into the sea. There was a narrow, connecting bridge of earth left. We humans walked it, migrating to the center of the continent to forge a new society based on non-duality.

When I awoke I was sore from sleeping on the bench. To my astonishment my mother and my younger self were looking right at me. They spoke to me about my dream, which they called a movie, for dreams in the afterworld are movies for the dead.

My dream movies had made me visible, and yet they still did not know who I was. "I doubt there could be a society based on non-duality," my mother said, "but I really enjoyed the cinematography." My younger self said, "Yeah, in your movie, even though California fell into the sea, when all the people walked together to the center of the world to make a new society, I felt happy." I wanted to take credit for the dream, but it was none of my doing; I didn't even remember it that well. The only thing that mattered was that though they didn't recognize me, at least my mother and younger self now saw me. (It seems life can change you so much you wouldn't know yourself.) "Your smile is familiar," my mother mused. "You remind me of someone." I was just going to tell them who it was when she said abruptly, "Let's go now," and turned away.

We ascended a spiral stairwell at the center of the station. We came to the roof of the station where tables and chairs and waiters and eaters were scattered all around. Some people sat on the ground singing. Others sat on the ledge of the roof with their legs dangling down, nervously looking around. A wall, the inside façade of the station, played films: the dreams of the living, a constant festival for the dead.

The musicians from the ferry played accompaniment. So much music. Mother explained that music gives the dead patience, "the highest virtue." A waitress came with dainty bowls of green gelatin, which I found both satisfying and delicious. I partook, forgetting the warnings against eating the food. As I ate, my younger self began to flicker in and out of view. With a jolt and a flat, echoing sound like an enormous lid closing, she vanished. My mother cried out and held my head in her hands, pressing her forehead against mine. In eating the food I had inadvertently closed off the passage back; now she knew me.

***

My mother would wait as long as she had to; there was nothing to do but wait. When I first arrived—shall I say "long ago"?—she thought I had the message she was waiting for.

She wanted to know how my siblings were. I couldn't tell her much. After her fall everyone had scattered, and I was younger by ten years than my nearest sister. Life had quickened for all the members of the family, and we sped along, doing our best to keep pace, but in one arena of the family's past, where our lives would always overlap in memory, life did not quicken, rather it remained absolutely still, as if not to be seen.

The statement *What we cannot speak about we must pass over in silence* had proven useful to us. For if a subject won't yield any understanding, then what is to be done? A family naturally gives up on the insoluble, the unanswerable, the hopeless cases—they are like fossils or mythology. Even if they involve local events within common memory, such subjects are practically Paleolithic in their random (lonely, common, exilic) indecipherability. Though perhaps "subject" is not the right word for this part of no speech, an unpredicated, empty space.

Families are experts on such rifts —between event and memory, between all sides of the story, the living and the dead, childhood and everything else. For the Spokes, the subject of our silence formed an unacknowledged nucleus around which we orbited with backs turned, looking out at the universe, sometimes sideways at one another, but never inward. If history brings us all together, secrets dwell on the underside of it, beyond the remedy, reach, and solvency of speech.

Call family secrets species of silence, except they are mineral, not biological but calcified.

I imagine a skull buried under a mountain, or a box with a rusted lock at the bottom of a pit.

The right accounting might break the lock, for perhaps that which can be honestly reckoned with can change— that is, whereof one can speak, one updates the subject; things can look different in the light—those things that we can talk about are subjects subject to change: They change under discussion.

But as with fairy tales, myths, political campaigns, and legends, what if it mattered more who spoke and when than what they said? Isn't it more important to be believed than to speak the truth? Haven't we learned from politics and circus barking that speech is not for truth, but rather for manipulating perception? Or haven't we learned from placebo effects and folktales and art that if only specific people, or substances, give the sought-after effect, it doesn't necessarily follow that this is because they are what they seem to be, but only that their seeming to be overcomes our doubt?

As so many villains and clowns have discovered, it is not enough, or even necessary, to say the true words.

The book, the charm, the dagger, the amulet, the enchanted animal, the weather, the genie, the god, the witch, the princess, the dragon, and the frog that are unleashed/ revealed/ conjured/transformed/disenchanted/ animated/ deactivated or released by magic words require that the right person speak them at the right time. The season, the hour, the garb, the stars, and the record must be in order for the magic to work. Sometimes the impossible is the missing ingredient.

***

If my mother was waiting for a message, for my part, I had a question. I kept forgetting it, though; I forgot for ages. And when I remembered I had a question, it was another age before I remembered what it was. It was like reaching for something but not having long enough arms. I reminded myself: Next time you remember your question, ask it right away. That is how it is around here: You have to remind yourself to remember.

And finally I did remember. And I did ask. At first she equivocated: "'Why?' is not a spiritual question, Lucia." "I don't care," I said.

"It wasn't a hard trick." "The Möbius strip? It's not exactly easy," she laughed. She put her arm around my shoulder. I waited. "Why wash those bones?" she asked. "What's done is done." "It's not done," I insisted, "or why would I be here?" We sat in the latest of her long silences.

I saw it all again, vividly, a welter of images like overlapping nightmares, the crowd in the round, her liquid dexterity as though drawn in the air by mercury, glinting in the shins, you couldn't keep track of her limbs, and then, absurdly, the beam of waltzing light that was her solo, as if she was slapped out of the air, reddening on the black Marley floor. I have stared my whole life at that image, captioned: *It isn't what you think.*

The grief never diminishes. It's just gradually obviated by the persistence of the present tense, the quivering copula between disasters. How are things moving and yet so static? I wondered, involuntarily witnessing for the thousandth time in my mind's eye her reverse flight.

Suddenly Silver spoke, saying, "Imagine walking all together on a dock over the ocean on a foggy day. We come to the end of the pier, and everyone turns to go back. But I seem to perceive that it continues; the air clears and I see a bridge ahead. I'm curious, so I keep walking. Eventually I find myself here. But for those left behind, I simply fall off; I am gone. And I was gone, for them. Two different realities, coexisting more than theoretically." Something thudded through me, thick, fibrous, and dusty, an old animal running from the answer I didn't want: that it had not been a fall, but a capitulation.

She seemed to backpedal. "It was an accident and an expression of purpose." But those aren't the same at all, I thought; she's confused. Is it possible that even she doesn't know what happened? "That makes no sense," I said cautiously. "I know," she said, "it wasn't what I thought." "What wasn't?" "The future—it wasn't ahead of me." "You're making no sense," I said. "So you've already said. But that is a good way of putting it," she said. "I lost my human sense, and that is the only way of knowing for you."

But what way of knowing could there be for a human, other than the human way of knowing? Even in this so-called "afterworld," didn't I remain human?

"Were you that unhappy?" I asked. She said, "Life seemed unreal; a death-dream. In any case, it wasn't choice, but chance... We don't possess our selves, you know."

"What was the moment of death like?" I asked. "It's very quick," she said, "like an exhale. I remember the chaotic vertigo and the feeling that at last— it was done. How much simpler life would be, now that I was dead. No more feeling or feeding, hunger or rage. And no more patriarchy—no more of that five-thousand-year-old boulevard of crime." "Did you even wonder how the rest of us would feel?" "I thought death would be complete nonidentity: Who would there be to recriminate? But I was wrong—for though the drama of the body had ended, the drama of consciousness was by no means over."

She was not expressing remorse, exactly, though some- thing had shifted. Not just between us, but all around us. She did not even possess herself, or so she said: How could she have been mine then, to lose? Or could one belong more to others than to one's self?

Who, what was I mourning? How to describe that loss? She was one thousand birds in migration; tired light; warmth, depression, and curiosity. She was real emptiness. But so am I.

"What was it like in between life and death?" I asked. "It wasn't really like anything," she said. "But even like has to be like something," I said. She thought it over and said, "Then it was like the back of the head seeing the back of the head in Magritte's mirror, or the earthen body traces of Ana Mendieta, or Godard's faceless conversationalists. I was bodiless, yet looking at something looking. Though it isn't quite right to say 'looking' or even 'I': I became a fiction. Or at least 'I' seemed to be only a barely extant device with which to see myself not seeing myself. Where was my mind? I can't say. And I'm not talking about that cabbage of pleated irrigators in our head, that network of custard and lightning, the brain. You know the joke about looking for a black cat in a dark room in which it is not? It was most like that. Though if I didn't exactly see her, I could still hear the cat—I mean I couldn't locate the mind, but I could echolocate it."

There was a knock on the door. My mother went to answer it and in strode the god I had seen earlier—bright brittle big jaw. He gave her a notice informing her that she had mail waiting for her at Nancy Spero's Tongues—the message station in the Liminal Quarter—and he left.

On Chrysanthemums of Hunger and the Reckless Moss of the Body

Karen An-Hwei Lee

If only finches, phoebes, mourning doves could say –

rice exploded in our foundling avian gullets. *No, this is a myth.* Is arsenic rice not carcinogenic, not a choking hazard, not a harm to birds? *Conserve rice at your wedding in light of the famine. Do not throw the rice. Say a prayer, instead.* Ask each grain of rice to shed its invisible wings, metamorphose into a fig-eating beetle. Or use shelled sunflower seeds. Say *Chryso* for gold, *anthos* for flower. *Chrysanthos.*

A cyst blossomed as if rogue cells roared freely out of a cavernous nocturne of starving moths: rapacious, not emerald lunas perched atop your summer-screen, over stick-bones dug up in a pear orchard. In beds of goldenrod. Phlox. Digitalis. Columbine. Born mouthless, a luna moth requires no nourishment to elope – analogously, chemotherapy starves the body in an oxymoronic healing. Born without a mouth,

a luna moth
fasts one week to sate desire—
    reckless moss of the body.

On Eschatological Radio Angels Flying in the Troposphere

Karen An-Hwei Lee

Millennial engineers of faltering air, not eschatological radio angels tighten struts, bolts, and cantilevers of eternal design. Angels guard antique equipment, invented in principle by our original architect, logophile, and alpha-omega *abba.*

Shoulders of unseeded rain encircle the troposphere,
    sweet jaggery of ferns.
Northern lights, the auroras, riff magnetic jazz above the poles.
    A low-frequency hum

                        signals human civilization or vice versa—

The long winter salts a tangible road of devotion. *Please tune in.* Do you hear me? Radio angels neither hunger nor thirst: *Tune in.* Desiderata of violent coronal flares, gore-jewels of salvation.

No one sees who is there
—lights on
            hovering afield.

Leaving Meshach

Chika Unigwe

The day Nani left her husband the mist that had earlier covered the morning skies cleared, the mild harmattan wind scattered plastic bags around her feet. There was nothing to suggest that something momentous had happened, except that her heart beat so quickly she thought she might faint. As she neared the part of Enugu where traffic was slower and houses had shrubbed fences and carefully manicured lawns, she slackened her pace. Instead of mechanics' garages and hasty zinc constructions lining the streets, here there were flowers and trees with pink and purple and yellow blossoms. Even the air seemed different. It was unhurried, generous. Obiagu was a concrete jungle: houses built so close together they seemed to stand on each other's toes.

She had almost forgotten that Enugu was beautiful and hot. Sweat dribbled down between her breasts, behind her neck, puddled under her armpit. Her throat itched from thirst. She still had three out of five bags of pure-water that she had bought from a street hawker peddling them in a wheelbarrow. She removed the sweater and stuffed it into her bag. She drank one bag of water, splashed the second one on her face and neck. Her eyes fell on her feet. The state of them - dry and cracked - Her mother would say; "Thieves' feet." As if you could tell the character of a man from their feet. As if everyone with soft, moisturized feet were epitomes of goodness. Her husband, Meshach had soft, baby feet. He was meticulous in keeping them soft, first soaking them in hot water for several minutes, and then having Nani scrub them with a pumice stone, rubbing the bottoms in slow circular motions while he directed her.

She didn't have much to fill the duffel bag hanging from her shoulders. Meshach had forced her to live a spartan, austere life. What weighed her down was inside of her. No bag would be big enough to carry it. But now, she hoped to discard that weight, shed it bit by bit, until she once again became that Nani who teachers had said was so light on her feet she could fly.

"You should run for Nigeria. With the proper training, you'll make a superb athlete," her sports teacher had told her.

If he saw her now, she thought, dragging her feet - where the burden inside her settled - as she walked, he would not recognize her.

Number 47 Osumenyi Street was home. And there she was returning, sweaty, damp under her armpits, heavier and more broken. Her feet cracked and her knuckles calloused. So exhausted from the long walk she regretted not taking a taxi. But on sighting the house, the heaviness lifted. This must've been how the Israelites felt on seeing the promised land. After seven years with Meshach, she couldn't even make a comparison without referencing the Bible. Her lips, too, were cracked from the harmattan and felt like sandpaper to the touch. She regretted having rushed out without dabbing some Vaseline on them first. But she feared that any extra minute spent at Meshach's would coat her in a viscosity that would make it impossible to leave. Her sister instructed her to leave. Leave immediately. She said go straight away home. She would find peace in her childhood home, as if peace were a surprise birthday present Ugo had hidden waiting for Nani to discover, the way she used to do when they were children.

After being gone for seven years, the affluent essence of Umuomam Estate had not changed. Even from afar, houses wide and huge, spread out like laundry hung out to dry. Satellite dish masts floated like ghosts above the roofs. The road to the estate wound past the private secondary school Nani went to. Protected by its high fence with barbed wire edges, through which, as she walked past now, she could see students in the familiar pink and blue pinafore running around, blissfully unaware that life didn't always unfurl in the way one wanted. Thinking of it now brought a familiar tightness to Nani's throat. She hadn't cried since this morning when a neighbor she hardly knew sat her down and got her thinking. "This man don' suffer your body plenty. Look at you? Fine girl like you? Why you let someone sit on your happiness like that? Why you let someone chop you so like mango?" She did feel like a mango, sucked so dry that the fibres had turned white.

The school bell rang for the end of break as she reached the gate leading into the estate, as if signaling the end of her life with Meshach. Or the beginning of a new life without him. With sudden, unexpected excitement, she saw herself working in a hospital, a stethoscope around her neck; imagined herself stretched out in front of the TV, a glass of wine by her side after a long day's work, like her mother used to. Ding! Ding! Ding! Each ding, Ugo's voice telling her: Leave. Leave. Leave. Her feet obeying. Ding! Ding! Ding! Her pace increased. Once she walked in, she swore to herself, there would be no turning back. This was it. She stopped, looked around, took a deep breath, and as if she was diving into water, she held her breath and walked in. The heaviness - as heavy as ice - which had suffused her body, fell off completely, dissolving and gathering in pools of water around her feet as she exhaled. Again, she felt like the Israelites in the Bible and resisted the urge to kneel in the middle of the road and kiss the blessed ground. She didn't want to attract any attention. But who would recognize her? Even her own sister had been shocked at her appearance the last time they met two years ago.

The houses on the estate were big and opulent, with wrought iron gates. Uniformed men on guard. Unlike the other houses, house number 47 had changed. Nani imagined it to be a stately, beautiful mansion with wide, sliding windows, but it had transformed into a big, rambling object she barely recognized. One window had a crack which was plastered over with duct tape. Her mother, punctilious to the point of obsession would never have allowed duct tape on her windows. It looked like somebody else's house now. The outside was no longer the dark chocolate brown of her memories - a color chosen by her ever pragmatic mother for its ability to absorb the dust of Enugu and hide it - but the dull, stained yellow of a decayed tooth.

In all the time that Nani was gone, she had never once passed by the house. She never even came anywhere near the estate. At the beginning, she couldn't have come even if she had wanted to but much later she still didn't. Had it been embarrassment or fear which had kept her away? In any case, what would she have come back for? She had lost touch with all her friends. Nobody she knew seven years ago was still around. Nkiru, Ugo told her, lived in Canada now. Montreal. The Ejimofor twins had moved to London. From their Facebook posts Ugo could tell they were doing well. Nani certainly did not recognize any of the security guards and so far, nobody had recognized her, or they would have been at the door. She was grateful for that.

The house looked bigger than it did when she lived there, as if it were dough rising and expanding, spilling off the kitchen counter. She wondered if it was magnified because she had become used to small, narrow spaces. Rooms so small that she could not stretch out without hitting something or walk without stumbling - like one walking in the dark - into one of the many objects crowding it: a suitcase, a table fan, a Bible. And shoes. Childrens' shoes. Men's shoes. She had kept hers under the bed, hidden from view, and would have kept everyone else's under beds too but those were crowded as well. Pots. Pans. Bags. The house spawned more things than it could contain, cluttering every nook and cranny of it. When she saw the children stumbling and falling into the chaos, and was helpless to pull them out of it, she closed her eyes and imagined she was back home. But this trick which had worked for her in the past, the magic carpet which could take her far from the cluttered house in which she could not breathe, did not work once the children joined her. They had never been to number 47. To be here without them, now under these circumstances, felt like a betrayal.

They would return to Obiagu Road, expecting to find her waiting, having no idea that she was gone. They would call for her and search for her, shouting "Mamman? Mamman?" But she would not be there to love them with her hugs. They would cry for her and Meshach would be the one to hold them and tell them,"Shhh. Stop crying. Papa is here! We do not need Mamman." They would be comforted. He would make them shriek with laughter and forget that they were missing their Mamman. They were children after all. The heaviness that she had shaken off earlier began to sneak back in. She could not do this. But she had to do this. Even if she longed to have them with her right now one day soon Holy, PraiseHim and GodsOwn will run around in the front yard at Number 47. Her chest felt heavy. She swallowed to force down the lump forming in her throat. She must not think of the children now. She had to escape.

The guava tree by the gate was gone. It was now a stump with tiny mushrooms growing wildly all around it, an amputated limb sticking out of the earth. Who cut it? It couldn't have been her mother, whom she and her sister had never got out of the habit of calling Mommy. Or Mommy Superstar. She loved that tree like a child. In turn, the tree had been faithful to her, producing baskets of sweet seedless guava which she liked to peel and freeze. Her daughters made fun of her. They didn't know anyone else who peeled guava or who ate the fruit frozen. She didn't mind the teasing. Not about the guava or any of her other strange habits. Her usual response was that if she sat around waiting for other people to endorse her ways, she would lead a sad life. Her mother made her own rules and tried to teach her daughters to do the same. But her mother failed spectacularly with Nani. She defied the poor woman's belief that confidence was something one could pass on, like fair skin or thick hair. Her mother's excess of self-confidence spilled onto her sisters bypassing her middle child completely. If Nani had been just a little bit more like her mother, she would never have found herself with Meshach. Confident people - like her mother, like Ugo, like her sister Udodi (before she died) were not soft around the edges as she was. They were capable of being nice but their niceness had a quality of assured hardness to it. Nobody could take advantage of them.

Nani noticed that the bench which used to stand beside the tree was gone also. Perhaps, it had been stolen and was now outside another house, accommodating the weight of other people who had no idea what role it had played the day Meshach turned up. Meshach, she spat; a dirty habit which under normal circumstances she abhorred, but which now seemed appropriate, as the name curled into her mouth and settled on her tongue like sour milk.

She slipped the key into the padlock, turned until she heard it click, and pushed the gate open. The gate had become arthritic and creaked loudly as she closed it behind her, pushing against it with both hands.

She had been carried through these gates when they still swung open noiselessly. She was about eight years old and had gone walking round the estate with her father, Doda. She must've stubbed her toe or something because Doda had to carry her back. The guard's room was open and she looked in, as if she expected to see his wiry frame. The room was empty. Even though it had been several years, she felt guilty about the guard and the punishment he suffered for letting her go. But she allowed herself only a moment of self-reproach. Old newspapers and rodent droppings carpeted the floor. Obviously, Aunty Enuka who came in regularly to check on the house and to frighten potential squatters away had not been in the guard's room for a while.

Although the jacaranda tree still dazzled in its blueness in the front yard, the orchard in the backyard - her mother's pride and joy - was now a sprawling graveyard of broken things: a kitchen stool; a magazine rack; a baby swing. Nani spied something that looked like the decapitated head of a doll. It rolled over when she nudged it with a foot, and two plastic blue eyes stared out at her from a dirty, smudged face. It looked as if someone had tried to burn it. The sight of it triggered a memory, the smell of burning hair deep in her nose. She was here to pick up the shattered pieces of her life and make it whole again. But how could she if she kept walking into memories.

Goose pimples crawled up her arms and she half walked, half ran, dragging her bag behind her back like an indolent pet to the front of the house and through the front door, into the parlour where so much of her childhood had unfolded. But this had acquired a new smell: the sickly sweet odour of something wrapped and locked away in a suitcase full of mothballs - specifically camphor - for many years. She could not imagine where the smell came from. Her mother never even used camphor. The smell disgusted Mommy.

The rooms - despite smelling different - had retained their colors but the effect was muted now. No longer bright and shiny and electric, so that Nani's father - whom they all called Doda because for some reason, that was what Udodi, the oldest child had called him from the moment she could speak - complained that he got a migraine from being inside and why couldn't Mommy Superstar have used such bright colors for the outside of the house instead of inside where he couldn't escape it? It was like the sun shining in your eyes, he said. The walls looked almost timid now, shrinking violets of colours, not daring to show their faces. Nani had expected to be comforted by the familiarity of home but nothing was as she remembered it. It wore the look of one that had been abandoned for years, accumulating dust and grime, yet it had only been two years since her mother and Ugo left.

Nani had not been in the house more than five minutes when her cell phone began to ring. She glanced at the screen. Ugo. Seven years had changed the balance of their relationship. Nani was older but anyone listening in would not have suspected that. Ugo, two years younger sounded like an older sibling.

"Have you bought your ticket? When are you coming?"

"I've only just arrived. I've left him. Isn't that enough? I've left, Ugo."

"It is not enough."

It did not surprise Nani that her first step on the moon was not a huge one for Ugo. Her voice was smooth and confident and boomed as if she were standing next to Nani and talking right into her ears instead of being a continent away.

"It. Is. Not. Enough." She had always been the stronger one. "It is. Not. Enough. How can you think that it is? Nani. It is not just yourself you have to think about! You are not 17 anymore. Grow up!"

Her words, sharpened and carefully aimed, did not miss their mark.

Nani took it silently and waited until Ugo's tirade died down to say, "I have heard. We'll talk later."

She could get angry but she understood Ugo would never deliberately try to hurt her. She was forthright but it was a forthrightness tempered always with kindness. She didn't have the ability to be malicious. Nani had shocked her sister with her story. She was determined to get Nani out of Meshach's house. Ugo believed that people could control their fate, that consequences were determined directly by actions. But Nani knew that it wasn't as simple as all of that.

Ugo had shrieked, "He did what?" each time Nani carefully served a part of the story to her sister and then Ugo repeated her words, "You said he threatened to burn you? Actually lit a candle and brought it to your hair?"

. Ugo didn't even know the entire story. Some stories form a tsunami of words and drown one if allowed to spill out at once.

Ugo pushed and pushed and pushed Nani until she did what she had thought she was incapable of. She packed the life she had with Meshach into her father's duffel bag and walked headlong into the future Ugo was charting for her: First stop, house 47. Next stop, America.

"I am just catching my breath," Nani told Ugo from inside house 47.

"You'll catch your breath in America. Plenty of time for that. It is toxic for you to stay there, to be so close to… to..." Ugo's voice was tight and packed. "Nani, leave this minute. How. Did. You. Get. To. This? Leave!"

There was no space for Nani to snake in. When they were younger, their father nicknamed his youngest daughter, Ugo the Stubborn, the "stubborn" soaked in tenderness. Nani was the Peacemaker; always afraid of confrontations.

"I cannot leave for America. Not just yet." She thought of her children and left the rest unsaid but Ugo responded as if Nani had said it anyway.

"You're stronger than you think. You can. You will. Look what you've done already. Mommy and I have been talking..." The mention of their mother spoiled Nani's mood. Why, she thought, could her sister not talk to her without bringing their mother into it? She pretended that her reception had gone bad, and shouted Hello! Hello! into the phone, shouting above Ugo's own insistent "I can hear you. Can you hear me?"

Hello! Hello! Nani drowned out her sister's words, and then groaned for good measure, complained about the poor reception, before hanging up on Ugo. Almost immediately, the phone started to ring again. A ringdringdrindring that pierced through the silence of the house. She threw it in her handbag to bury the sound. She was drained. Forty minutes it had taken her to walk from Meshach's to the estate. Forty minutes in the sweltering heat but she did not care. Every part of her ached, but there was no point to freedom if it was painless.

Two Poems

Angela Karee

#

I am mother
of a feared thing most
Dark scrawl
of it(s) body
like a pen inked dry
as I'm writing this. *Why*,
my precious? Why *my* precious
? Such a natural thing—
such like the natural
winds and rains and flames
that rip the natural limbs from a God's
man made things
to make study of

These ones heirlooms
of incriminating marks
from birth turning under the Sun
more black
Blacker, still
til they're ashen

'til they're lightless
          And by then
                    it don't matter

Ask me after   if I'd have
     spread my legs   far wider
than I ever had before
     And beared down at all
when the island-tinged woman
          in her festive wares warned:
                    Not yet, honey, you'll tear

Aubade

Last night was the last night,
but who could've known?
Your normal's broken open—
the bright yellow morning
sprawling to a noiseless, numbing gray
that'll only end when you do.

Your baby spilled
onto the sidewalk, beneath the window
from which you've called him—my god—
a million times home,
before the streetlights, the thunderstorms,
the shit brewing on the corner hit the fan.

You, knowing of nothing else to do,
take the cold throne because it comes naturally,
but skip the breakfast meats and coffee,
pull on some clothes, ghost
down the stairs and out the front door.

This day could have been the start of anything.
There are tires on the surface of the roads,
shoes and the bodies that fill them pressing on.
There is everything in defiance of the new reality:
a city late in waking, cold and grimy as ever.
A world one boy short.

Oh, to see you in the shadow of this soft sunlight,
prostrate on the concrete,
trying your damnedest
to siphon him back home.

Memorial Daze (It Takes A Lot To Laugh, It Takes A Train To Cry)

Kim Dana Kupperman

"Each time we remember something specific . . . that memory grows stronger. Like a path through the woods that grows more defined each time we walk it. If this is true though, what then does it mean to forget?"
—Maribeth Fischer, *The Life You've Longed For*

I. Poppies Will Make Them Remember

During a walk through the woods on Memorial Day, I am thinking of poppies—their hot, maddening, unalleviated, scalded red—and the fallen soldiers they commemorate. I am thinking, too, of Moina Belle Michael, who in November 1918 experienced an idea as revelation: "In a high moment of white resolve I pledged to KEEP THE FAITH and always to wear a red poppy of Flanders Fields as a sign of remembrance and the emblem of 'keeping the faith with all who died'." Michael says she drew inspiration from the famous poem, written by Colonel John McCrae in homage to a fallen friend at the Second Battle of Ypres, which begins: "In Flanders fields the poppies blow / Between the crosses, row on row," and ends "We shall not sleep, though poppies grow / In Flanders fields."

But say the word *poppy* to anyone who might have read L. Frank Baum's *The Wonderful Wizard of Oz*, or seen the film of the same name, and the association might conjure Dorothy and the Cowardly Lion overcome by the narcotic power of "a great meadow of poppies," drugged by the wicked witch to make them forget—albeit temporarily—their mission. If the fantastic story of a girl and her companions—on a long walk through a mystical kingdom—had inspired the Remembrance Poppy, would it have had the same meaning?

If Moina were walking with me now, I might say that in spite of her "high moment of white resolve," once you use a thing to symbolize something else, its original meaning often becomes unremembered. In fact, neither Flanders nor fields have ever crossed my mind when I bought one of those poppies sold outside grocery stores by veterans or members of the Ladies Auxiliary, the folding tables lain with literature and sometimes home-made baked goods, the women invariably in well-ironed, practical dresses, the men wearing hats on which are pinned medals or embroidered names attesting to their status as soldiers.

When I see those faux poppies, my thoughts do not turn to Belgium or the Great War, but to my neighbors who have seen battle and what they never say. First my nephew and his tour to Afghanistan in 2003 at the start of this mess in which we are currently embroiled. Then Jimmy Aronson, the son of my mother's cousin, who did three tours in Vietnam, a nineteen-year old who tolerated my ten-year-old-girl crush. I think of my father's dog tags, stowed in a case, and that he never said much about the war in Korea. And the scores of soldiers addicted to opiates because of pain resulting from severe injury, and how their addictions tell one story and conceal another. I want to forget the cruel irony that many of those men and women are still being wounded in Afghanistan, a country renowned for its opium trade.

II. It Takes a Lot to Laugh

Memorial Day was once called Decoration Day and originally honored the fallen soldiers of the Civil War; the holiday was celebrated on May

30th.

I know many military folk won't like hearing this, but given that we've already twisted what Memorial Day commemorates, perhaps the holiday should honor anyone who has ever died for love—of country or turf, another citizen, an ideal, or just the freedom to walk in a street or drive on a road. That we should decorate the tombstones and gravesites and crime scenes of the oil slicked, the IED'd, the suicided, the domestically homicided, the overdosed, the succumbed to AIDS, the lost the battle with cancer, the stroked, the heart attacked, the shot down by gangs, the killed by police, the murdered in schools, the sniped on patrol, the massacred in schools and places of worship and dance clubs , the slashed and burned, the run over, run down, electrocuted, lethally injected, tortured to death, the assassinated. That we do not forget any of them, not the soldiers missing parts they fail to forget but cannot retrieve, nor the children who played in the love canal, nor the women brought to their knees.

III. "Then I'd comb my hair and throw away the poem . . . / this poem, in the trash"[1]

Late May and the woods are renewed with wing and song. Red-winged blackbirds chattering in the pond reeds. Cardinals in the maple tree. Pine boughs sighing and the echoed coo of mourning doves. The promise in the stretching light and warmth that the hummingbirds will arrive any day now. And then the feeling that all we're really doing is hanging onto this beauty, as if for dear life itself.

Which is one reason, perhaps, that in spite of the luxury of the almost-summer birds and all this green and feathered beauty, I am queasy. I'm not sure anymore what it means to be a Jew, especially in the comfort of America, when the Palestinian, "expected to forget he's

---

1 Mahmoud Darwish, "Remainder of a Life" (trans. by Fady Joudah).

human, is forced to accept the exclusion from human rights that will train him for freedom from forgetting the homeland."[2] To remember a homeland—to yearn for the quotidian practice of language and tradition—is, of course, the quintessential prerequisite for being an immigrant. But the Palestinian is a refugee in exile on the edge of home. Exile is a condition intrinsic to being Jewish, though Israeli Jews seem to have both forgotten and not forgotten this. When the birds forget how to migrate, we will be even more lost.

But another wound fractures my thoughts and threatens to widen into grief: the image of a two-and-a-half-foot stack of poems that my friend Robert told me he left out with the trash. He is a tall man, and I picture him tilting his head to listen to the garbage truck as it rattled down the street, then peeking out the windows to watch as the "sanitation engineers" removed his stack of verse. Wondering then, wondering still, if that disposal was the right thing to do.

What would make a man, one who cherishes words, consign his own to a landfill? To unsound all those syllables, unbuild all those stanzas, unwrite all that language, unstitch all those hours: what kind of courage is that, apart from being a valor without measure, that goes unrecognized on Memorial Day?

Four years later, Robert sends me a photograph of his best friend. In the picture, Sam is about nineteen. He is sitting on a foot locker, his head resting against his hand, his gaze direct, expression seductive. He is holding an M16 with a peace symbol painted on the weapon's butt. The light is a faded gold that is typical of old photographs. "I call it Born in the USA," Robert tells me. Sam has just committed suicide.

IV. "The law of the past cannot be eluded"[3]

---

2 Mahmoud Darwish, *Memory for Forgetfulness.*

3 Walt Whitman, *Leaves of Grass* (To Think of Time).

And what, really, are we supposed to remember on this day? The price of war?[4] The unsolsticed, faux beginning of summer, when ladies may once again don their white shoes and jackets? Hamburgers and hot dogs and the national diabetes epidemic? That our appetite for grills, dandelionless emerald-carpet lawns, and twenty-four-hour Walmarts is backstory to the Deepwater Horizon disaster in the Gulf of Mexico, an event I can barely stand to contemplate years later, because when I do, the picture of an oil-drenched brown pelican[5]—which I simply cannot *unsee*—frustrates any attempt at compassion I may have for the eleven workers who died in the explosion on April 20, 2010.

One image bleeds into another: the blobs of oil—"like melted chocolate"—washed ashore at Grand Isle, Louisiana, the setting of Kate Chopin's novella *The Awakening* (whose title should be considered a prescient announcement of what we *must do now* to prevent such disasters from ever happening again). I see, again, images of those petroleum-soaked otters of Prince William Sound in the aftermath of the drunken-boat horror of the Exxon Valdez. Over twenty-five years later—a generation, in human terms—if you dig on those Alaskan beaches, you hit oil. The body does not forget.

V. "...to reconcile / the people and the stones."[6]

Robert, whose poems are now disintegrating in a landfill, once made a pilgrimage to the home of William Carlos Williams, only to discover

4 According to a study in 2013, the cost of the wars in Iraq and Afghanistan will total four to six trillion dollars. "Every hour taxpayers in the United States are paying $4 million for the cost of war in Afghanistan [and] $117,035 for the cost of war in Iraq." See: http://bit.ly/2cUtj7u

5 A bird that was removed from the Endangered Species List only six months before the Deepwater Horizon disaster.

6 William Carlos Williams, "A Sort of a Song."

that the blue rock in the garden (where the poet sat and contemplated things) had been demolished, the stone put out with other "remodeling" debris. Robert furtively "rescued" a piece of that broken rock. "I wish I had a garden to put it in," he told me.

What stones shall we set in the gardens we have not yet planted on this Memorial Day? One for the heroes of the burning towers? One for the suicide bomber? One for the child lost, another for the amputee? One for the black life that mattered, one for the cop working his beat? One for the student or teacher or club goer?

In his dispatch from Beirut during the August 1982 siege, the poet Mahmoud Darwish writes, "Anti-forgetfulness wars; anti-oblivion stones. No one wants to forget. More accurately, no one wants to be forgotten."[7]

VI. Those Who No Longer Remember Who You Are

How might we reconcile ourselves with the too-heavy-to-move stones of our Alzheimered memory?

On this national day of should-be remembering in a country obsessed with forgetting the genocide on which it is founded, the lessons of history, and even age itself, let us now remember the elders who waste away in places we once called nursing homes and which we now refer to as Assisted Living. Think of it: To live with assistance in a nation whose citizens value so firmly their independence. Or, at least, their interdependence. One such resident of these newfangled homes was my father's sixth and last wife, Mary, one of thirteen children who grew up speaking Yiddish in the Bronx. Eleven daughters and two sons. When their father died, all the girls in the family worked to put the two boys through school. Mary is the last one alive; widowed twice after my father died, she has endured the loss of everyone who is truly familiar to

7 From *Memory for Forgetfulness*, p. 15.

her. "I am lonesome," she tells me as we sit in her rooms at the assisted-living facility run by Marriott.

On this side of the complex lingers a faint smell of antiseptic detergents, the worn skin and bones and flesh of the aging, and the recently sprayed scent of Febreze. We mask the odors that make memory. We box up our old folks in buildings run by corporations. All recollection erased.

When we go to dinner, Mary tells me about the activities at the facility: musical acts (what lurid covers of "On the Boardwalk" last played here? I wonder) and crocheting, visits to the beauty parlor, occasional outings to the movies. She says that she doesn't tell anyone her true age (ninety-four) because she's older than most of the residents and is in excellent health (still cunningly beautiful are her legs, which, along with those of her eleven sisters, were famous—"those Schulman legs," people called them). She has no dementia and no diseases. Just a few aches and pains, she says. Unlike the majority who live here. But, I think, all of them are in the process of departing, with scant recording of their lives and memories, without so much as a question as to what they recall about wars or the soldiers in their families, or what fruit was available in the market when they were children or how the loneliness of being forgotten has really affected them.

VII. Go Shopping

And don't forget the Memorial Day Mattress Event. The Buy-One-Get-One-Free Offer. The Super Sales. The 72% Off Deal. Just look for the giant American flag flapping outside the store or the mall. And if no star-spangled banner waves above these depositories of our disposable income, or if you've misplaced one of the many circulars[8] delivered

---

8 Read: the never ending stream of junk mail whose production, distribution, and disposal (or recycling, if everyone were to recycle them), consumes another

through the postal service and you're in a tizzy about where to find a nearby sale, there's a website that can help. Shop till you drop and just forget about what it once meant to remember.

VIII. Hit the Road, Jack

On Memorial Day weekend 2010, just after the Deepwater Horizon disaster in the Gulf, an estimated 32.1 million Americans took to the road; hundreds died and more were injured; close to half of the holiday fatalities on U.S. highways involve drivers who consume alcohol. Experts at the Automobile Association of America said they could not predict what effect the BP oil spill would have on tourism that weekend, but everyone in the Gulf area pretty much expected that folks wouldn't flock to their oil-slicked shores.

As of this writing in August 2016:

- 6,879 U.S. soldiers have died in Iraq and Afghanistan[9]
- Some estimate that 1,000,000 soldiers have sustained injury
- According to National Institutes of Health researchers, some 320,000 veterans from these wars have sustained brain injuries[10]
- 22 veterans commit suicide every day[11]

---

deepwater well's worth of petroleum.

9 Source: http://antiwar.com/casualties/

10 See: http://www.ncbi.nlm.nih.gov/pmc/articles/PMC4255273/; see also the work of public health researcher Rachel Chase, who discovered an alarming rate of undiagnosed traumatic brain injury among veterans from the wars in Iraq and Afghanistan: http://magazine.jhsph.edu/2015/spring/features/invisible-wounds/

11 This particular number has a context. The source of this is comes from: http://bit.ly/1mbwVuQ; see also: http://lat.ms/17N0fqk; http://wapo.st/1M4BpBL

Between the point of my writing this and the point of you reading it, more soldiers will be wounded or die. The shortest distance between two events is as large as a death, as small as a metal shard disrupting a person's brain, as far away as Iraq or Afghanistan, places most Americans cannot identify on a map.

IX. What Is Not Forgotten

Walking in the woods, it is hard to forget that squirrels remember where they hide each and every one of the hundreds of acorns and nuts they bury.[12] Birds remember the twists and turns of thousands of miles of flight paths to and from nesting sites.[13] Walruses depend on their whiskers to identify members of their herds; rhinoceroses make urine mounds to communicate with one another; elephants memorialize their dead by passing the tusks of the departed. Dogs recall things that frighten them.[14] Cats pretend to remember nothing, though they are very practiced at the ritual of following the sun as it moves through the house.

---

12 According to Dr. Pierre Lavenex at University of California at Berkley, gray squirrels, in retrieving each nut from its singular burial spot, "use information from the environment, such as the relative position of trees and buildings, and they triangulate, relying on the angles and distances between these distant landmarks and their caches" (cited in *Animals in Translation*, by Temple Grandin).

13 The migratory route for Arctic terns is 18,000 miles round trip.

14 But as Temple Grandin writes, "Both animals and people can 'get over' a learned fear. But getting over a fear isn't the same as forgetting a fear. Extinction [a term used by behaviorists to describe the phenomenon of extinguishing a particular response to a stimulus] isn't forgetting; it's *new learning that contradicts old learning*."

X. One Memorial Day (May 2010)

Early morning light saturates the woods where I walk, attempting to remember something important that someone said to me, or whether I told a particular story to a particular person. I rummage around my mind for names of people I went to school with, streets I once lived on, things I did that seemed inconsequential but weren't. I try to recall a dream. In the spaces where those memories once resided, I leave imaginary pebbles, memorials to the unremembered trivia of my life.

I try to envision—to *recall* in the present, as it were—what it must be like for a woman in Afghanistan to not only survive without education or rights but to live under a burqa, to have her entire self hidden to everyone except other women, her husband, and her immediate family, how hot it must be under that stifling mandate, how anonymous to the point of breaking, how tiresome.

XI. "Do you think I could walk pleasantly and well-suited toward annihilation?"[15]

To complete an average day without weeping for hours on end, I must consciously forget that which wounds the psyche. For example, I do not want to remember that, for a time following the Deepwater Horizon disaster,[16] an amount of oil equivalent to the Exxon Valdez disaster continued to flow into the Gulf of Mexico every *six to twelve days*.[17] I

15 Walt Whitman, *Leaves of Grass* (To Think of Time).

16 10.8 million gallons. Or one gallon a day for approximately 29,589 years.

17 The oil that that continues to gush into the Gulf may well cause the kind of food-chain collapse inherent in an extinction event. Unfortunately, though, we are not talking about the type of extinction that animal behaviorists describe; the human animal has not yet alleviated its fear of living without petroleum.

have no desire to recall the predictions that mitigation of this damage will require five generations to pass.[18] By then, who will remember the names *Exxon* or *BP* or *Valdez*?

And then the news that we may never leave Afghanistan because major deposits of lithium—worth a trillion U.S. dollars—were rediscovered there.[19]

Like any human living in these times, I would protect myself by not dwelling on the fallen-in-war, the slaughtered-by-the-error-of-human-hubris, the crushed-in-cars, the extinguished-by-murder. Yet these dead linger on—preserved in minute-of-silence newscasts on PBS, in the CNN or Fox News crawls, in obituaries, on radio shows, through headlines—and in these constant parades of names and reports, those who have perished simultaneously vanish, dying a second time, forgotten again.

XII. Forgotten Elegy: It Takes a Train to Cry

No train stops at Gettysburg, where I once lived, though there are railroad tracks and a train station. Which means that to claim the bodies of Sergeant Jonathan E. McColley and first Lieutenant Robert

18 Five generations means that if you have children, maybe your great-great-great grandchildren will be able to see clean water in the Gulf of Mexico. Which means you cannot take your children there or your grandchildren or even your great-grandchildren. But maybe you think more like George W. Bush, who, when asked by journalist Bob Woodward how he envisioned the future, responded, "Well we won't be here to see it."

19 The Russians knew of these mineral deposits. The Afghans hid the maps that detail where they were located. Which begs the question of what intelligence really is, given that the American intelligence community surely was aware of the maps (and thus the deposits). Rediscovery is an odd use of tense and time, especially given the ancient country we're talking about here.

A. Seidel, III (two young men from Adams County, Pennsylvania, who died in Iraq), their families will have to travel somewhere else. There will be no kin or neighbors assembled along the railroad tracks as the train pulls in bearing the bodies of the fallen because no train comes here anymore, to this town where the Civil War turned and where trains once stopped. No flag-draped caskets will be carried from the station to the funeral home.

Let us now praise these not-famous young men, whose faces are broadcast on television and computer screens, whose deaths are only virtual to those of us who did not know them, whose brief imprints in homes and lives and towns and places beyond our imagination were too brief. Let us now observe a silence for all the other men and women who have perished thusly or been transformed beyond recognition. Let us now walk in the shoes of the other—be it the Palestinian if you are a Jew, or a secretary in the World Trade Center if you are a jihadist—and listen to our enemies. Let us now remember, every time we start a car, the disaster in the Gulf of Mexico, and let us also recall, when we proclaim cleanliness next to Godliness, each and every creature, from the tiniest shrimp to the burliest man, inhabiting or working those petroleum-poisoned waters. Let us now unearth the words in the landfills, set the rock in the gardens, and assist the living to tell their stories.

Lest these truths, which we may have forgotten to hold as self-evident, be unremembered.

Suicide Subtly

Janeil Page

A few years ago,
I fucked a student in my office.
Any suicidal thoughts, the psychiatrist asks?
I'd never considered the concept of regret
or reset—*No,*
not really, I reply. Though ropes
sound romantic, unless you break your neck
it's just too painful and too
wringing-chickens-on-Saturday-night
for-Sunday's-family-dinner
ablution ritual for my taste. Pills appear
pleasant, but without the know-how,
you're likely to become a vegetable, or end
with your kidneys hooked
to a Brita filter.
I'm no predatory pedophile,
just an adjunct at a college. He was
three years younger, twenty-six
and brilliant. He wasn't really my student
anymore, not for six months. *Irreverent*,
I'd called him.
We shared my Vicodin

but he didn't like the idea
of being someone who only takes.
I don't want this to be about that,
he said. We fucked on my lunch break
while people sat outside my door.
It must have been God who decided
that I would seriously malfunction,
that my body would always be
at odds with me and would do so
when I was twenty-one,
with two small children,
a bad husband,
one degree,
and no aspirations
beyond finishing another,
proving them wrong
about being ruined.
We fucked in the woods
while my children waited
with my new ex-husband for my return
from a morning hike. I brought back doughnuts
to explain the delay.
He said he would ruin me, that boy
of mine, because he was broken,
because he believed
I was such a good girl before him.
I wonder how long it would take
for Lupus to kill me. *She died*
of the complications of Lupus,
they'll say. And for pity's sake,
I could never do anything

melodramatic. I want to make a pretty
corpse, which rules out drowning
and guns. Bleeding out seems good, but gory,
scarring. I don't want to be someone's bad dream.
In the past, I would go a few weeks
without taking my meds,
a month at most. But suicide is not passive
in any manifestation.
It can be, the psychiatrist says. I wonder how long
it would take if I started today?
Flannery O'Connor was forty-seven.
They gave her five years tops,
but it took fifteen. Her father was thirty-eight.
My aunt, from cancer, was fifty.
He said my night class students would only know me
post-coital, red-faced and messy.
We fucked without condoms.
He told me I didn't have to do it.
He knew me well and this wasn't me,
but he was only a voice in my ear.
Another pregnancy could possibly
kill me. An opportunity
I'd never considered.

Eyes of the Tiger

Janelle Poe

Saturday night at Le Tigre and a fight is coming on. Harlem is hot again and this is a good local restaurant. Modern French bistro near 116th, just off the main strip so not as much foot traffic as on Eighth Avenue, but still a nice place with great drinks and food, nice people. We have our regulars, a few birthdays, and the first-timers who just happened in. I rarely work Saturday nights but our weekends are typically low-key. Not tonight. The energy is charged, which is optimal for business, but it's strange to see this much commotion over a fight. Two muscular men prancing around topless in shiny shorts and sneaker boots, pounding their fellow man to pieces? I can understand the allure back in the day, *before* satellites, before cable. Back when there was only one movie theatre in town, during the Golden Age of radio, but now? I only pretend to care because it's hospitable, that's what bartenders do.

"Welcome to Le Tigre." Keep a warm smile, make eye contact. "My name is Rose, yes, yes…ha, ha…just like the wine, but not quite…Named after my grandmother…Yes, it *is* perfectly French." Keep smiling, place menus lightly and pour water. Add lemon, straws. "Here's a list of our cocktails. I always recommend the Monseigneur, bourbon with an herbaceous twist or the Piaf, champagne with hints of grapefruit and elderflower." Two of our most popular drinks and the simplest, therefore fastest, of the seven house cocktails to make. The others require muddling, rendering pulp with herbs. Look—a full bar and nearly the entire restaurant—almost fifty people here and everyone's drinking. Those cosmopolitans, mojitos, margaritas, vodka tonics and martinis are my responsibility. Rum and coke? But what type of rum? We have several varieties.

Offer but don't push. People are more agreeable when they have choices. Smile through the exhaustion.

Been on my feet all day, since boozy, bottomless brunch and the dinner rush is steadily approaching. Marco, the only other bartender called out, via text, forty-five minutes before his shift started. Nice. I was supposed to go home but I need the cash. Rent's due and my college roommate, Kamara, is finally getting married. Her bachelorette weekend's in Vegas next month and airfare's a stretch, much less bridesmaid duties.

Francois, the owner, acts like I barely know what I'm doing but he practically begged me to stay, rather than cover the shift himself. I watched him sweat while I debated, as if the money wasn't worth working an unplanned double. He offered me dinner from the menu instead of family meal *and* priority on next week's schedule. After tonight, I'm actually off for *two* days. First consecutive days in weeks.

"Merci beaucoup! Thank you! You're the best. La vie en Rose!"

Oui, oui. Je sais.

I savored every bite of the hanger steak and pommes frites while the rest of the waitstaff tried not to look envious as they pushed around gargantuan roasted duck wings in a soupy red sauce over rice.

Stop and stretch. That twenty minute break was the only time I've sat down since brunch. My back burns and so do the balls of my feet after standing for hours, tedious despite wearing sneakers to cushion the lugging, carrying heavy crates of bottles and supplies along with cases of champagne up from the basement closet and walk-in fridge. Up and down rickety stairs, up and down behind the bar. Clearing plates, grabbing glassware and flipping bottle caps. Squeezing lemons and limes, slicing. Bending, squatting, pouring and shaking. Straining, topping and tasting, concocting Bloody Mary mix, batches of sangria and four kinds of mimosas. I'm approaching ten hours, with four, maybe five more to go with this fight. Twenty bucks an hour in tips is not enough and the hourly wages scarcely cover taxes, but I can walk to work. How many New Yorkers can do that? Sometimes the work feels repetitive but the atmosphere is always changing, besides Francois lets us drink during the shift, within reason.

Generally steady, Le Tigre's moderate pulse is manageable, but when the rush happens: Showtime! Energy spikes—fractions and digits, seconds to greet, ounces poured, pounds served— right down to the cent. Although the pressure can be crushing, a Jefferson never quits. Except when it comes to bartending, according to my parents: "We didn't pay for *four* years of college so that our *thirty-five* year old daughter could work somewhere that doesn't require a *high school diploma*." I come from a long line of hardy individuals, traceable through slaves and sharecroppers, maids and bellhops, to soldiers, seamstresses, and now an executive and accountant. Before bartending I was corporate, most recently three miserably stagnant years at Willes, Inc., a "top notch" boutique agency where my ideas were constantly stolen and regurgitated by others who were rewarded for my labor. When my HR complaints were deemed "inconclusive," I left that world behind. Besides, we're not meant to spend the majority of our lives sitting under artificial lights in poorly recycled air. The Jefferson family sigil is a man struggling up a steep mountain, dwarfed by a colossal pack and shoeless, but head held high, looking up toward the glistening summit; I'm simply continuing the tradition.

"J'adore Le Tigre! C'est parfait!" A charmed customer remarks. "Curry mussels, s'il vous plait." She's adventurous, this one.

Clean white walls against exposed red bricks and chunky wood are comforting, the reclaimed zinc bar in vogue. Contemporary graffiti artwork hangs with gilded mirrors and traditional French cinema posters. An Eiffel tower wine rack assembled for good measure, subway tile in the bathroom. Black and white faces all around, dissolving into cafe au lait and pastis, brown and lighter brown, paler by candlelight. Bleached, starched napkins splayed on country wood. The scene is pastoral, for Harlem's resurgent gentry.

There are so many couples in here tonight. Date night, in all its iterations, keeps us afloat. It's been eight months since my last date, certainly far too long for my age. Love should be in motion by now. I'm no supermodel but my skin's smooth, I have a great smile and pretty eyes. On top of being educated, I can cook and take care of myself. No roommates. I shouldn't be out here still looking.

Kamara and her man were together for four years after seeing each other off and on for nearly a decade. Blending lives takes time and there aren't even any prospects. Come July, I'll be attending another wedding by myself.

After the last two floundering internet dates, I've sworn off virtual connections. My friends think bartending is the perfect way to increase my romantic options, meanwhile my mother thinks I'll be pegged as an easy girl, potentially an alcoholic. So far, most of the men I meet here are already involved or drink too much and ask creepy personal questions, turning sad and then belligerent, or vice versa. Behind the bar, the delicate balance between being personable and getting too personal is difficult to maintain. Speaking French can lead to intense discussions about my being African-American vs. African-African—and six white customers have tried touching my hair.

Seat one-fourteen is glaring at me murderously, a lion to an impala, gnawing on her bread as she might my femur or bicep. Pre-empt the standoff with remorse. "I'm sorry that your appetizers are taking this long. I'll check on them right now." Refill their glasses liberally, "These are on the house." The woman's pale face is drawn tight into a frown. It hasn't been *that* long but I deliver an apologetic half smile that indicates genuine empathy and embarrassment at the delay, without any trace of irony or sarcasm.

Since I'm alone, leaving the bar is dangerous and costly. Jean-Marc, the runner, bursts through wooden country doors. The slatted panels swing back and forth from his force. Francois is red-cheeked and sweaty in the steamy kitchen, now its own giant oven. Pots clang, oven doors open and slam. He yells in French and the chefs are focused, flying. Cramped in small quarters, I doubt his fervor is helping, but this is what he does. His nose is bright red, as if he's been punched in the face. He might actually be drunk from brunch.

"Don't go in there," says Jean-Marc.

Luckily he has my dishes in hand. Anticipate, anticipate, "Thanks," I say. "And more bread for the bar, seat one-fourteen, when you have a chance?"

"Okay," he says, the food runner's accent sharp and lovely.

Present the plates proudly, luxuriant pâte platter to the left, luminescent herb-dusted tuna over avocado on the right. Precisely prepared and executed, the dishes should be worth the wait. "My apologies again. Cracked pepper? Enjoy."

After their first bites the customers relax into their seats. Smiles crease the corners of their lips, *We are winning*, their faces flash and reflect. Now they resemble the couple at one-ten who are definitely on a date: two handsome men, details bespoke; sharing laughter, toasting their vibrancy and enjoying each other's company. Fresh ginger and rum with a splash of soda and lime, absolutely complimentary I think.

Making my way down the bar again, there's a trio of good-looking brothers in the corner. Animated, the new arrivals are thrilled to have found a spot at the bar before the spectacle begins. Lightweight jackets and sweaters come off, revealing solids and plaids, sturdy physiques, defined chests and biceps, a golden flash. My heartbeat quickens.

"Besides track and field, this is the most classic of sports," says the handsomest one, as I place menus before them. His eyes are striking.

"*Classically* barbaric," I retort. "The Greeks and Romans have a pretty sordid history."

He laughs. "Didn't your father teach you about boxing?" His left eyebrow is raised and for an instant I'm caught in the kaleidoscope of his iris, flecks of emerald and beryl glinting against the dimmed lights. Scrunching my face to indicate that he should know better he laughs again. "You're funny…and smart. I'm Claude," his hand crosses the invisible plane between us.

Setting steaming glassware out to dry, I use a scratchy white towel before touching him. "Rose," I say, returning the firm shake.

"Like the flower." He's still holding my hand. Slightly moist palms, the pads are calloused and I wonder how they became so thick, no rings. I've seen him, at Le Tigre and randomly at other Harlem spots. He's the Red Rooster, Corner Social type; always well-dressed and enjoying himself, attractive companions nearby. Claude and crew are the best-looking and hopefully unattached men in the room and I am not the only one who notices. "This is Luke, and this is Omar." His friends sound like Harlem, their greetings confidant, demeanor suggestive. They look like Harlem, Washington Heights, the Bronx, at ease in crisp short-sleeves, designer tees and dark denim, coordinated kicks. Claude's light eyes and walnut tone, combined with his friends' medium complexions and curls point south, to the Caribbean. Maintain composure, witty banter. Pour their twelve-year scotch neat, walk away.

"How's my makeup?" I ask Sophie. "Haven't been to the bathroom in hours."

She smiles approvingly and I'm grateful. Sophie's mid-western, a bi-racial beauty with a killer downtown aesthetic and though she's younger, she's an avid reader and audiophile, into modern art as much as trap and the blues, so I trust her judgment.

"Homeboy over there is all about you. Watch out now!" She nudges me in the shoulder and hands over several orders, which are quickly piling up as the fight is about to begin.

"Girl please," I reply. "He just wants free drinks."

Sophie sucks her teeth. "I think he wants some rosé," she says, before excusing herself through the crowd with a tray of drinks and water pitcher, the pepper mill tucked beneath her arm.

Smiles all day and all night. Even when people are rude, like this man in the back, frantically waving his champagne flute. I smile in acknowledgement, hoping he will stop flapping as if he were flagging down a tow-truck or rescue aircraft. Mid-bite, a heavy-set bald man in front of me asks, "Is the fight gonna be on tonight? Should we stick around?" Apparently he couldn't read the chalkboard outside. Reply emphatically so the customer knows that Le Tigre can meet all of their needs.

When I was little, my father and I used to watch boxing together. My back against the black couch, I sat on the shaggy carpet in the same position as when my mother would braid my hair, minus the comb being yanked through knots and medicinal green grease applied to my scalp. He'd drink whiskey or beer and I would have grape juice, sometimes in a glass mug like his. We'd eat nuts, bowls of them. Cracking pistachios open, using our teeth to break the smooth pale joints, and the flesh. Crunching on potato chips, a salty treat for a Saturday. He told me all about the glory of Muhammad Ali and Foreman, Sugar Ray Robinson and Smokin' Joe Frazier. We watched Sugar Ray Leonard, Holyfield, and Tyson, world champions who showed everyone the undeniable power of black men.

"Look at their stamina, the prowess," my dad would say, admiring their strength and ability to do what so many others could not: beat the *White Man* down, take back their manhood, then swagger victoriously. Never mind the blood, the missing teeth, the concussions, or the fact that they often fought one another instead. The heavyweight damage done to the fighters' bodies and minds always seemed worth the money, the praise, the heft of the garish golden belt nearly too heavy to hold above their heads at the end of the battle.

I enjoyed spending the time with my dad, seeing his joy and excitement. For once, not feeling sorry that I was his only daughter instead of a son. But as I grew older, all the aggression, the vicious tension between blows became disturbing. Crowds roaring and jumping up from their stadium seats, peering down into the arena pit. Spectators taut like rubber bands, as if they were the ones delivering the punches, ready at any moment to turn to their neighbor and deliver a right jab to the face, a left hook to the chin. Knockout. Television made this type of violence acceptable, celebrated even.

Clear those plates at 101. More water at that two-top in the middle. Smile. Smile. "Another cocktail?" Turn on the dishwasher. Lemons are running low, and limes too. "I'll be right back with your check… Your entrees should be out any minute. Something else to drink in the meantime? Please don't ma'am…let me put those olives on a plate for you, it's more sanitary." Lights flicker, candles. Cue Stevie Wonder. There's a birthday, *clap, clap*.

Peter, the Maitre'D is talking to a party of four that just entered, hoping to be seated tout suite. Reservations must be full because he's sending them towards the bar, where standing room is extremely limited. Complimentary glasses of champagne on the way, my duty as well. Ladies first, grasping clutches they switch sleek purses beneath the weaker arm so as not to spill, shift their weight and accept the drinks. "To Saturday!" Clink. Light toss of long straight hair, pursed lips, a sip. *We are winning*, they beam. Creamy, sun-kissed shoulders held effortlessly straight, looking like late July when it is only May. The men lag behind, oblivious to the servers trying to pass by. They toast and immediately look up at the flat screen, now playing pay-per-view, then back at each other. "It's the fight of the century!"

At the other end of the bar I can feel Claude, his eyes on my body as I rush to complete these tickets. I am at work. I am on display. I am a professional. Measurements just so, but the jiggers are cumbersome and I have to keep rinsing the tiny metallic tools. A click of the wrist, recently incorporated double shakes along with the music that has changed from stomping Motown oldies to the pulsating thump of house. Muddling is unavoidable—mojitos, mojitos, mojitos.

In the background, fervor builds as commentators trade facts, point out flaws and weaknesses in the contenders, wax nostalgic about previous battles. Le Tigre is jamming and the room is buzzing, the men especially, laughing loudly and pounding each other on the back. A glass shatters, briefly puncturing the din then levity resumes.

Sangria and beer need replenishing, soon I will have to go downstairs. The door might be locked. Where's Francois? At the circular table in the back, by the bay window, drinking with his friends. He's cracked the door with the wrought-iron handle and bars, but the air cannot reach me. He kisses his fiancé Melina. She pushes him away. He laughs, he drinks and returns to the kitchen.

"Mayweather,— right?" A unanimous decision amongst Claude et al, but his tone suggests a test, questioning my blackness.

"Of course" I reply, stacking the old-fashion and collins glasses in the least precarious of possible formations. Pints and martini glasses set to chill. It's true, I want the brother to win, but the matchup bothers me, what their bodies represent. Black versus Filipino, dark versus light, "exotic" prize fighters facing off in a cage, on an American stage.

"That's my girl," says Claude, raising his glass. But I am not his. His laughter rings deep and his smiles last, posture straight and assured, comfortable with his stature and the attention. Even the black woman in front of me with a fine man by her side, to whom I was invisible, is sneaking glances while she scrolls through her phone. In a different world, I would be on the other side. I would laugh at Claude's jokes and break out all my meaningless sports trivia to impress him and his friends. Only now is not the hour of fantasies, it is time for more shakers and ice.

Bells clang and the melee has begun. All attention shifts towards the screens suspended in opposite corners of the wall behind me. There's no time to watch, not even to analyze our crowd based on which contender they root for, to examine the implications. The scene is frantic, a blur of cupped fists, blocking or augmenting outbursts, brand labels on the bottles I handle and the caps flipped to the floor, measurements and mixtures, garnishes. My movements are non-stop, nearly automated as I complete tickets, tend to the guests in front of me, enter orders and close checks, trying my best not to be rude or slow. Everyone is waiting for something or someone, and that person feels like me. Isn't this fun?

***

After several rounds, groans and yelps punctuate the crowd at Le Tigre and there in Vegas. Eyes glitter, so many lights sparking eagerly in the night, Claude's included. He winces and *oohs* along with the others as Mayweather lands several heavy blows to the forehead, temple, chin while Pacquiao retaliates with a flurry, connecting with belly, skull, ribs. The room explodes but soon the cheers dissipate as frustration builds. Perched on their seats, the people want more action, more food and drink, complain that nothing is happening. Demanding blood or a knockout, their cravings will be satiated, somehow. The fighters' rage is dispersed throughout the room and voices are raised, a couple argues in the corner. Hopefully there won't be any brawls.

"Is the kitchen still open?" The tickets do not stop. Recipes rush down from my brain into cups. I pour and ice and shake, nearly cut myself twice. Finally there is a lull in the orders.

"Quit all that dancing and knock him out!" someone yells, and the room is full of laughter and accord. Sophie taps her fluorescent watch and nods toward the door. My first break in hours.

Outside is my only escape and I can finally relax. The weather is nice, slightly crisp and refreshing. I cannot remember how many drinks made, corks popped, checks presented. People seem happy and are tipping well, I have worked hard and we have nearly made it through. *We are winning.* Soon we will tally the score.

There's applause while I'm outside and when I return, the fight is over. Bruised, both fighters look stunned until announcements are made and Mayweather struts to the corner of the ring, climbing the ropes to elevate his stature and pose with certitude, arms crossed and daring dissent. Remaining undefeated he is crowned the undisputed world champion, two enormous and detailed belts drape his shoulders. In Le Tigre, the mood is deflated and folks are complaining about the judges' point-based decision. There was so little blood, no biting, no knockout, no overwhelming defeat.

"Mayweather played around too much. That wasn't really a fight," says Claude.

"It's all about that paper. Why risk serious injury?" says Omar.

"It's about being the best," says Luke. "They should fight again."

"I could've danced around like that for two hours. Pay *me* one hundred eighty-million dollars. I got your Mayweather. Pow!" Claude two-steps with balled fists, punching Luke's shoulder.

"You can't be doing too badly," I add, gesturing towards the heavy black and gold watch on Claude's wrist. He laughs, raises his glass and we toast, Johnny Walker vs. Crown and Coke.

"Last call, last call," I shout. I can officially break down the bar.

Nearly done cleaning, I drain the rubber mats in the sink and toss them in the scratched gray bin alongside the other dirty, sticky implements. Francois approaches, exuberant and flushed. "What a great night, ladies and gentlemen! Thanks to you," he shouts, clapping loudly. "La vie en Rose! Let's have shots! And this guy, Ricard. You are the man!" He pounds the head chef, young Algerian guy, several times on his back. Ricard looks beat but proud.

Claude and Omar are two of the few remaining customers and the only ones at the bar. "Drinks for these guys too! Welcome to Le Tigre," Francois says, giving them dap. I set out ten shot glasses and hold up bottles of vodka or whiskey for those whose preference is unknown. Claude smiles at me while Francois proclaims, "To Fight Night!" We echo and drink.

The money is good, very good. More than I've ever made at Le Tigre and my daily total is well over five hundred dollars. Stuffing this cash into my bulging wallet feels triumphant, better than a digital, direct deposit paycheck. I earned this money with my mind, my smiles, my sweat and aching muscles. The crew carries the same blend of exhausted accomplishment. A sense of power and endurance, like running a marathon together. *We are winning.* Now we celebrate.

Sophie, Arianna, Jean-Marc, Christoph the busser, plus Ricard and a few of the chefs are going out. How could I refuse the gang? Not after such a long day. Thirteen hours flew by and I could definitely use another drink. *Les Tigres* fits us perfectly as we stroll down Eighth in a pack, loud and bubbly ourselves, though as one of the oldest, I hate to think of myself as on the prowl.

Claude and Omar are not far behind us when Sophie squeezes my arm whispering, "He's definitely interested. I'm actually feeling his friend—Omar, right?"

I nod and we smile, trying to play it cool. Peter, the maitre d' yells for us to slow down and no one can believe he's coming. We cheer loudly as he joins us. "Pedro, Pedro!"

At Silvana's, they greet us with high fives, hugs and handshakes. Industry folks take care of industry folks. "First round's on me!" I hear but can't see the voice. There's confusion at the packed bar and Claude moves closer.

"What are you drinking? It's my turn to take care of you." For a second I'm overwhelmed and unresponsive, feeling his firm chest against my back though we're barely touching. Smoky birch and dusty incense waft around me as I turn, looking into his burning eyes.

"Two Jamie's and ginger," he tells Amil, the bartender, before I reply. Amil tilts his head slightly, expecting my usual Crown Royal order but I don't want to embarrass Claude. Men hate to be corrected.

Now standing directly beside me, I try not to stare at his impressive profile, to get caught up in his height and how good it feels to be this close to such a gorgeous man. In sneakers, the top of my head is just below his chin and there's no straining to speak, even in this noisy place.

"Keep it open," he tells Amil, handing over a credit card and passing me the drink. I thank him and he raises his glass, "To the finer things." We toast and our eyes linger.

Claude makes way for us through the crowd and finds two seats on the wooden benches in the back. We sit and I push my bushy twist-out away from my face. The curls are shrinking in this humidity.

"I love your hair by the way," he says. Hookah smoke swirls and congregates on the ceiling above tapestries and handmade chandeliers. The mosaic of patterns and throws, people and sounds, seems as if we are somewhere across the Atlantic, closer to the equator than a few blocks north of 110th Street.

"So, how did a beautiful and intelligent woman like you end up behind a bar?"

This isn't happening, but it is. He's attentive as I give him the abridged, comedic version of La Vie en Rose: college in California, internship to entry-level position at the third largest ad agency in North America, back to New York, several smaller boutique firms like Willes, Inc., considering wider possibilities, like moving abroad. Women in revealing clothes and hooker heels stare us down while dancing nearby but Claude ignores them. Only once does he look away, checking on Omar, who's dancing with another woman, unfortunately not Sophie. His focus is on me and the intensity is returned, I can't look away either.

He is Guyanese, first-generation. Owns his own apartment, a pre-war hardwood that he refurbished himself. College-educated and well-read, he speaks English, Patois, and Spanish, knows how to build walls and tear them down, respects people who use their hands, good clean work.

Between drinks, we dance along with the Le Tigre crew. Christoph is hilarious with his ridiculous moves in the middle of our group's circle, and we are laughing, spinning, drinking. Claude looks me in the eye as a seductive pop song slows the mood, taking my hands and pulling me in. "I'm having such a good time with you."

I smile and enjoy the music, being close and feeling safe in his arms. When the song changes, he turns me around and pulls me tight, whispering, "I bet you do this all the time."

I stop moving and turn to face him. "I've never been this close to a customer."

"Well then, I must be special," he says.

"You are."

***

It is a little after three a.m. He lives north of me so we share a cab uptown. I am beyond tired, but buzzing from the alcohol, the cash, the night, from Claude. We kiss in the cab and his lips are soft but firm, his tongue is sweet. At my stop, he pays the driver. "I'll walk you to your door." he says. When I hesitate he squeezes my hand, "I'm a perfect gentleman."

The driver pulls off and I shiver, as the air is colder now. Claude wraps his arm around my shoulder for warmth. Just a little wobbly, but not drunk, I know what I'm doing even if he does come up. We're adults and he's not a stranger, we actually have a few friends in common.

Searching for my keys, he stops me again to kiss. When I open the door, he's right behind me. Shy, we wait for the elevator in silence but in the hallway he tells a funny story about locking himself in a client's bathroom. Inside my apartment he is complimentary, impressed by the color scheme and my paint job, the furniture. On the couch, he looks so good, arms and legs spread sitting back in a place no man has been in some time.

"Let me rub your shoulders," he beckons. "You were killing it behind the bar tonight…you deserve a massage." He kneads slowly, then firmly and again, his large hands on my shoulders are wide and encompassing. I melt into the warmth beneath the pressure. He pulls me toward him, his forearm tight against my chest and I quake. We kiss and before I know it my bra snaps undone and I am lying down while he hovers above, leaning on one arm for support.

He pauses after a while, leaning back. "This is uncomfortable," he says. Standing, he leads me down the hallway to my room. On the bed, I place my hands against his bare chest, "Let's take it slow tonight."

He smiles. "We will," he says, kissing my face.

It is dark and his breath is warm, ringed with coconut hookah and whiskey. Light kisses down to my navel. He unbuttons my jeans and I flinch.

"Don't worry, he says. "I know what I'm doing." Soon I'm floating, bobbing, weaving, lost in the waves. Then he is on top of me, above me.

"Sit up," he says, grabbing the back of my head and clenching my hair in a fist. He thrusts himself in my mouth and I gag. He pushes harder and harder, his grip tightening and I think he will rip out my hair. I choke and cough. He pulls away. "I knew you'd like it rough."

My eyes are wide open but I can barely see him through the tears.

Whimpering, the words scratch against my raw throat. "Stop, stop. Just go."

Grabbing me by the neck, he lifts and tosses my body to the side, like a doll. I try to grab the edge of the bed but he pulls my hand away. "Don't fight. You know you want it." He pounces on top of me and covers my mouth. I bang at him with my hands but he's a frozen mound of steel. "You didn't say please, you dirty slut."

My tears stream into the sheets and I wish they would swallow me instead, swallow me whole. I can barely move, he weighs so much that shifting makes the pain worse. He pushes down harder and I shudder, clenched and shrinking inside of myself.

"Stop," I plead.

He growls obscenities and pounds me into oblivion. Numb, rigid and frozen in place, I feel nothing, not even his hate.

Eventually he pushes off and wipes himself on my sheet. Coins fall from his pockets as he grabs his jeans, clinking to the floor. "Thanks for the drinks," he says while buttoning up his shirt. He laughs sharply and walks out, knowing I'm too weak to hold him there while I call the police. To scream bloody murder. The front door opens and shuts. Then he is gone. It is the middle of the night and who can I call? What would I tell them? Was his name even Claude?

"Officer help me. I've been robbed."

But he didn't take my money. Sore, I bury my head deep in the pillow muffling strangled sobs, wishing I could rip off my skin while tears drench cotton, sting my face. The idling bus on the corner departs and a siren wails in the distance.

A woman cries on the A

Aurora Masum-Javed

You want to hold her. You want her
to disappear. This is how you feel

about most people. She undoes
her hands, reaches the left

to stifle a breath. She takes
in so much, you worry

none will remain. You too,
are one to cry in public alone.

Where to put your eyes?
You think of your mother.

Her blue robe crusted with black dye.
The days she couldn't rise, weeks

she moved only for solitaire, mahjong.
Woman who lived

off String Theory, Darwin, feasting

on Cheerios, singing herself small

Bangla prayers, but she knew god
was a lie, and everything that wove,

wove between you. Silence—
a punishment, a freedom.

She had no one.
You had her.

*

On the train, you catalogue touch—
a father, his baby's sleeping belly—the only.

No one moves toward the woman.
No one moves toward you. You think

of the weight. The days you can't
and can't. How much you've taken

from your mother. How much she lives
in you. Her body

like your body
like this woman's body.

*

There is a pact we're not making.
Retreating as we do to our sterile machines,

void expanding. But think
what was made of small things

and a ruin of space. The moon,
debris made whole, stone

that stays and stays. Stay. Please.
I will inherit what you leave. Gravity

longing to collide. All of us
conjoined, mouthing *autonomy*.

Excerpt from Winter: Aphorisms

Sarah Vap

Drones are probably killing someone right now

Rub it mama. Kill it. Put sword on it thanks.

Every day all day long the babies kill, are killed, want to kill, admire the killing, fear the killing, enact the killing, pretend to kill, try to truly kill, think they have truly killed, think they have truly been killed, don't fear the killing, enjoy the killing, kill guilelessly, kill guiltlessly, kill effortlessly, kill with abandon, kill with zest, kill ambitiously, kill with stealth, kill with flair, kill thoughtlessly, kill as an afterthought, solicit killing, encourage killing, laugh at the killing, glory in the killing, kill many different ways, kill with many different weapons, relish the ways they might kill, revel in the variety of deaths they have experienced.

Drones are probably at the babies. Gentle people I.

Gentle puppy, killer, don't kill.

Drones are probably killing someone right now

Drones are probably killing someone right now

Let's kiss. Again. Again. Again no.

How do we not kill anything.

How do we extricate love from. How do we not become poisoned if we are poison I.

How do we come to love the poison. How do we get our hands on some poison how do I explain the rage I.

I am not comfortable with the amount of rage that has filled me since they have been born.

Do I have as much love as I have rage I can't be sure, my love is enormous I.

I try to move through this world with love/drones are probably killing someone right now—I think this thought relentlessly but I cannot understand it.

I can't think hard enough I.

Drones are probably killing someone right now

What We Love

Drones are probably killing someone right now

And stop fucking hitting your brother for the fucking millionth time today.

The rage is in inverse-proportion to the love I want to believe this.

I want to cry with the love! there is so much love and it is beautiful what is wrong he hit me in the face why because I put the sweatband on the cheetah.

When the babies came, the more the love, the more the rage, the more the drones.

The trafficking, the climate change, the more precarious the intimacy with the distant-close holes of the heartbeat.

The more precarious a shared world interior, the more tender the utterly.

That utterly enraged baby.

The more utterly tender the world the more utterly enraged. For the world I porous at tender holes.

Drones are probably killing someone right now

Drones are probably killing someone right now

If you love your babies without hating something else even more.

Grammy says we don't use the word "hate" in this family yes we do.

She says no yes sweetie we do use the word hate. We just have to hate the right things oh lovey that makes you sad.

Mateo of singing. Mateo of dimples and the lost front tooth. I'm right here and we're all in love.

Mateo holds my face in his hands, looks into my eyes, says: I'm not gonna let that happen to you.

Tenderhearted fierce Mateo oh.

Note found on my pillow: Hello Grouch, Meet the big gets-mad-at-every-single-thing. Her second name is "the inquisitive" and "must be precise about it all."

And that boy is so big now and we love each other you can't imagine how much and he is so full of love and rage I can hardly bear how wonderful!

Drones are probably killing someone right now

What We Love

Drones are probably killing someone right now

And we are all of us, as he says, in love.

Does this love give us strength or gaping terror, gushing at.

Orb, muddled views on so fast much I.

Alienation theorists and self-harboring systems I.

I don't believe it possible that you love your children if you don't also fall apart with your love for all the children in solitary confinement at Rikers.

If you don't have plans to burn down Rikers I.

I don't believe I love my children if my heart isn't also destroyed with love for all the people destroyed for our protections I.

Exclusively for souls I. Exclusively for souls I.

I hate you the world's shittiest white woman asshole just imploded with love of the world I.

Drones are probably killing someone right now

Drones are probably killing someone right now

I love yet cannot evade the question of whether he will absorb ethereal bodies of rotation inside me.

Open and fragmentary, or until broken apart at my soul-brains.

That child. And then, simply, the whole world.

Choose a safe online name. Use email addresses, IM names, chat nicknames, and other such names that don't give away too much personal information. Pick a name that doesn't help identify you or locate you.

If you don't look at your baby and think of Kalief Browder then you don't actually love your baby.

If I don't look at my baby and think of Kalief Browder then I don't actually love my baby.

Everything, even more than ever, not simply in pairs capable of reproduction.

If you're not always thinking about the drones.

Drones are probably killing someone right now

What We Love

Drones are probably killing someone right now

The infants sleep and break into their holier parts. The infants wake and congeal.

The infants asleep and awake across two years while Kalief Browder is in solitary confinement for allegedly stealing a backpack, also the drones that I cannot fathom.

Whales Deepwater Horizon and the murder of indigenous environmental activisits I.

Get that out of your mouth love.

I have found no way to say how sweet, how sweet, how soft and wet his little kiss is.

His wide open wet mouth he wants to eat my whole face with love and a devouring heart I.

The toes. The little fat legs. The bitty hands. The startle-reflex that needles also into my center-brains.

Drones are probably killing someone right now

Sarah Vap

Drones are probably killing someone right now

How sweet the strong suck, and how the babies find peace on my body.

How our smells. How their holy little minds. Their holy little bodies.

Their profound perfect tiny infinities, drones that are probably killing someone right now.

I imagine all the other babies of profound perfect tiny infinities and they amass toward me I.

My god I.

And they are already in all my smallest parts mixed evenly around I.

I am so fucking enraged and at whom and where can I direct the rage and what I.

The genius of late capitalism is identifying at whom exactly I am enraged and.

Drones are probably killing someone right now

Drones are probably killing someone right now

We are batter. Milk in the batter, milk in the batter, we bake cake and nothing's the matter!

Don't throw that block past the tower, throw it at the tower—check your trajectory. Our baby is on the other side of the tower from you when you throw the block from there so aim at it from a different direction.

Utter destruction can you say that Archie? Utter destruction then everybody laughing hysterically.

The primordial soup, struck by lightning and. Did someone just poop?

Use strong, unique passwords for every site to reduce the risk of someone breaking into your account.

Allowed to, or made to hurt in private.

The lines of distinction, breakage point, fracture, fault line I.

A hole. Filled with this person.

Drones are probably killing someone right now

Sarah Vap

Drones are probably killing someone right now

I have heard that when the wolf is actually at my jugular I will feel peace.

I am very glad for a wolf to eat me but not the. Now a tiger again raar!

The wheat inside the crop circles was burned by butane gas and my kryptonite hey she's writing it all down guys.

That river is a real river, that's the river you can always re-enter identically, that's the intrauterine river of omnipotence, immortality, and impurity.

But do you see how increasingly disordered and lumpy the properties are?

And then, if the lumps begin to rot, that's hope.

If there is hope, if there are feathers, then there are still drones.

Joy, and you can fall into it laughing hysterically. Passwords.

Drones are probably killing someone right now

What We Love

Drones are probably killing someone right now

Joy reveals a reason for aversions to sweetness, even the most harmless oral enjoyment causes something that will remain unacceptable for the freedom of the hero.

A hero is the mouth hole. Is that poop?

Who is the mouth hole and who is the asshole. Who is the nose hole the ear hole the eye socket the piss hole the hole they cut to lift you out of. The sweetness outbursts everywhere I.

I am a thermometer and we live in a cesspool.

Littlest baby's hot mouth sucks one nipple then he sits up and vomits on my other breast. The bigger baby also is hot at my back and we all become hotter into the night.

Babies are hotter and hotter and my nipples burn when he turns to nurse at night. The heat of their fever in their mouths wakes me when they nurse at night I.

Instantaneous terror then the.

Drones are probably killing someone right now

Drones are probably killing someone right now

Temperature of their ears, how many diarrheas, how many vomits, is there enough pee in the diaper or are they dehydrated and all at once they are all three sick. No one comes to visit us is that another diarrhea we better start writing these down.

2:30 am boy diarrhea; 2:30 am boy at 103.2; 2:30 am baby at 102.8; 2:35 am for boy ibuprofen; 2:55 am at 103.4; 2:55 am baby at 103.4; 2:55 am baby acetaminophen; 3:15 am boy at 102.6; 3:15 am baby at 102.0; 3:25 baby diarrhea; 3:40 am baby 102.0; 3:40; diarrhea

for the boy; 4:00 am 101.4 and diarrhea baby; 6 am 102.1. This goes on for days—.

Our heads. Our torsos. Who we murder while we tender for babies I.

What doesn't show.

Drones are probably killing someone right now

list of things to say instead of "i'm fine"

Marlin M. Jenkins

my blood moves like tectonic plates: so slow
one might not notice, but notice first, please,
before the earthquake.

i have always been afraid
of waves, how they say:
i know   *what it's like*
to crumble *over myself and*
hear my crashing simply
called   *beautiful.*

the syncopation
of my heart's swung notes
is more than   metronome. but
not quite a full song, either.

i woke up this morning
as a houseplant not watered
in weeks. when i tried

to move, wilted pieces
of brown flesh crumbled
onto the carpet, waited
there for the vacuum.

i am tired   of how this skin
makes lonely, how afraid i am
that i'll say i'm   black
and scared   and no one
will listen—that i will say
i am proud   and be
perceived therefore as threat.

today is that ice cube song,
but because a good day means
so much forgetting.

something in this city
is always on fire. before
the neighbor's car it was
the house around the corner.
before that, the trash can
on the curb the night
before garbage day.

remember playing *the floor is lava*?
like that, except the lava is also

the walls and ceiling and furniture.

maybe moses' feet were burned
when he removed
his sandals at the feet of the bush.
what saint has not lived
constant pain?

hansel and gretel left
bread crumbs when they should have
left a trail of blood,
held their faces down and
admitted they were lost.

i no longer have to meet yearly
with the cardiologist. i will not miss
the tug of ekg stickers pulling off
body hair, but i miss the jelly on chest,
the dull pressure of the instrument
pressing skin around ribs and sternum,
to see my center on a screen—
yes, there are parts in here
that are pumping,
working, despite.

Self-Portrait in Green (excerpt)

by Marie Ndiaye
Translated by Jordan Stump

2002 – Because it was in front of her house that I saw her each day, for a long time I couldn't distinguish that green presence from her surroundings.

I drove by, taking the children to school, then I drove by again later, now alone, on my way back, then twice more in the evening, going off to pick up the children and bringing them home, and each time, without exactly meaning to, I glanced at that old farmstead's front steps and barren yard, and each time my gaze encountered an undefined form that immediately after melded in my memory with the single tree on the lot, a tall, spreading banana tree.

Four times a day, then, I drove by her house. And I looked at her and didn't see her, and yet a vague unconvinced feeling always turned my head in that direction, though I noticed nothing, ever, but a lovely, surprising banana tree. I stepped on the brake as I drove past, almost at a crawl, and never once did my gaze fail to meet with the still, watchful silhouette of the woman in green standing near the far-more-imposing banana tree, and I know that beyond all possible doubt. Because four times a day my heart was gripped by something unnamable, though not absolutely malign, the moment I passed by the farm with the lone banana tree in its fenced yard, and then afterwards, all along the road to the school, in all sorts of yards, I looked at many, many other banana trees with the most perfect indifference.

But I like knowing names, and, convinced it was not knowing who lived in the farmhouse that was bothering me, I asked around. "Oh, that place? Those are just the X—s," people said. And it was a common name in the area, and belonged to many other families besides. There was nothing to be had from a name like that, nothing to learn.

One morning I stop the car in front of the house. I shut off the engine, pull the handbrake, then turn to my four children, three of them in the back seat and the oldest beside me in front. It's a spring morning, warm and glittering. The children's arms and legs are bare. Their hair shines. The windows are rolled down and the car is filled with the smell of honeysuckle, as if we are all wearing perfume. But my children's skin smells naturally of honeysuckle, their necks and their cheeks. I smile at them all with the playful squint that announces I've come up with a new game. They're still small. I whisper:

"Look closely at that banana tree. Is there something or someone anywhere near that banana tree?"

And each of my children looks toward the farmhouse, and their attentiveness, their docility, and their concentration, the utter lack of reserve in their obedience, all that brings me to the verge of tears. It's something else, too. It's also the nearness of that banana tree, of course, with its leaves so broad that any one of them could enfold my youngest child, it's also the imminence of a discovery. A golden dust floats above their heads. Their foreheads are curved and serene, their napes still pale. Have I mentioned this? My children's arms and legs are bare, because the air is warm, intoxicating.

They were a little disappointed.

"There's nothing at all beside that banana tree," they whispered.

"Sure?" I asked.

A shiver ran down my back.

"Sure," said my children, with unmingled certainty. I turn the key, put the car into gear, and start off a little faster than necessary, not taking a last look back at the farmyard. "You're the one I need," I begin to sing under my breath, and when I check the rearview mirror just to be sure, I can see that my uncalculating, unafraid children are happy, they've already stopped thinking about that big banana tree. They're not thinking about the desolate farmhouse, they're not thinking about what they didn't see near the banana tree. We drive slowly, alone on the little road, in the odorous breath, warmer with each passing moment, of a gigantic mouth. That's how I see all this, but I keep it to myself.

"You're sure?" I asked my children, my spine suddenly cold.

And since my children never delight in deceiving me, how could I not believe them? But at the same time, how could I answer that I myself had just seen, had just for the first time made out, beside that banana tree, a woman in green? How could I tell them I found it hard to believe they hadn't seen that woman in green just as clearly as I could now see her, her who until that morning, I realized, had eluded not my eye but my awareness?

Then I said to myself: that woman in green has always been there. She's there every morning and every afternoon, beneath that banana tree, and she watches us creep past her house, and she sees me looking at her without seeing her.

What I don't know is: is she waiting for me? Does she somehow resent not being seen, does it somehow frighten her, or is that just what she wants?

I realize that my children are still in the first stages of this phenomenon, where I myself was stuck until that radiant spring morning when I first found myself seeing a woman in green in her graceless garden, a garden she seems to occupy only at intervals, when it suits her, a garden whose bleakness and blighted look she's surely not to blame for.

The woman in green is there, every day. Is she still there when I'm not around? I obviously can't question my children about that. Or can I? My children, with their bare legs and perfect arms, are utterly without guile. Anything they believe, anything they sense, they'll tell me.

I pull up in front of the school's lilac. The lilac is covered with little white flowers, and all at once their honeyed scent fills the car. It's almost more than we can tolerate. I ask my children if their heads aren't swimming a little, as mine is, and they answer no, and I sense that they don't quite understand the expression "my head is swimming." Other children come crowding around the car. Some put their heads through the windows, bringing with them a fresh gust of lilac, and I worry it might nauseate my children. The others' legs and arms are also uncovered, their limbs are plump, their skin packed tight with hard, dense meat. Every one of these children is friends with my own. All smiles and darkly glinting braces, their faces are puffed up with excitement, with joy, with the many anticipations and unexplored wonders of the day just begun. I feel relieved. I look at those children with an affection full of gratitude. I feel relieved, swollen with kindly thoughts. Before my children get out of the car, I put on a sly voice and ask:

"If you see someone whenever you go by his house, does that mean he's there all the time, or only when you go by his house? What do you think?"

My four children sit still for a moment to ponder. Then they shrug apologetically, all together, to signal I've asked them a question they can't possibly answer.

Now they're out in the schoolyard, and my two youngest stand glued to a spot beneath the plum trees, with that wavering look, that vaguely lost, uncertain, disoriented air that often comes over very young children when they suddenly find themselves alone amid shouting and jostling. Seeing that makes me melancholy. I'd like to walk into the schoolyard, take them by the hand, and drive them back home. I can't help thinking it's wrong to desert them like this, but I know that's a wrong, dishonest feeling, I know they know perfectly well that they're not being abandoned, not being consigned to some horrific fate. I remember my own fright when I was their age, I think I can remember that, and that's why a lump comes to my throat when I see such young children alone on a vast, raucous playground. Still, what are they thinking? Are they sure this day will end? That they're not stranded here, alone among dozens of frenetically active bodies, for all eternity? They know, they know. Is that certain?

Then a disturbing memory comes back to me: I remember a woman in green from my grade-school days. Tall, brutal, and heavy set, she promises us all a trip to prison if we eat too slowly, if we dirty our clothes, if we don't raise our eyes to meet hers. Her eyes are green, and she matches them with long checked skirts and turtleneck sweaters. Because of her, a pall of dread hangs over the school. She carries more than one child off toward a dark hallway, proclaiming that prison waits at the far end, and cries of terror resound as that stout woman disappears with her little prisoners clamped beneath her green-sleeved arms. The children are never seen again. They must have been seen again, surely, and yet it seems to me that they never come back, that their two tiny chairs sit empty in the classroom, and that this is the natural way of things, terrible and coherent. They hadn't behaved.

And my two little ones, under the Japanese plums, do they behave?

Now they've all gone inside. The schoolyard is empty, the sweet lilac has numbed me. I must have been one of those children the woman in green carted off down an endless hallway, but fear and the inescapability of the torments to come kept me from crying out. Was I ever seen again? It's true that green can't possibly be the sole color of cruelty, just as green is by no means inevitably the color of cruelty, but who can deny that cruelty is particularly given to draping itself in all sorts of greens? Before going on my way, I pull three leaves off the lilac and slip them into the pocket of my shorts. That might come in handy, I tell myself, though for the moment I have no idea what's awaiting me.

All the young women are in shorts, because it's a shimmering spring morning, and in the amber air there's an imperceptible threat of the sweltering summer that will unavoidably follow this season, so mild and at the same time heavy with that warning— it's a wall shining bright white in the blazing sun, for example, or a shadeless gravel courtyard I cross through on my way into the town hall, the baking heat already contained within those four walls enveloping me in a way I've forgotten. All the young women are in shorts and sandals. The sandals' soles smack their heels with a certain resolute gaiety. What makes that sensual? Is it the slightly slack strap that lets the foot slip this way and that, and the heel slap the sole? Or is it the vision of unveiled legs? What makes it sensual, and must the legs be beautiful, must they be lustrous, smooth, and long? Or is the beauty of legs, knees, and ankles superfluous for the burgeoning, in the main street of this drowsy town, of an eroticism still enfeebled by winter? Is all that possible in a town this far removed from the breeziness, the rustle, the hum of the city, is it possible?

All the young women were in shorts, that dazzling morning. Leaving the town hall, I walked with long strides in my army-style khaki shorts, perfectly pleased to be who I was in that place—the main street of a humdrum little town—and at that time, and this contentment was crowned by a vague surprise at the very existence of such a plenitude, the conceivability of such a pleasure. That's when I run into Cristina, but as soon as I see her I'm not sure it's her rather than Marie-Gabrielle or Alison. Not that her name escapes me: it's just that, among those three women, I no longer know which this one is. Deep in my pocket, my fingers squeeze and shred the little lilac leaves. This person who might be Cristina is a young woman, so she's wearing shorts, elastic and clinging, with a print of green flowers against a green background. My elation dwindles a little. It occurs to me that wariness might be called for. And yet I like the idea that soon I'll be driving once more past the house of the woman in green, and she'll be standing there, knowing I'm going to stop. But Cristina's shorts are something else altogether, because I hadn't expected them, and because green isn't the usual color for women's shorts, in the first days of spring, is it? Cristina keeps her hands behind her, pressed flat against her powerful hindquarters to display her shorts' exuberant color as flagrantly as she can. She stands with her legs commandingly spread, blocking the entire width of the sidewalk. As luck would have it, she keeps her sunglasses on, and I've forgotten what her eyes look like, or Marie-Gabrielle's, or Alison's. Her blond hair is pulled into a ponytail so severe that the skin on her temples seems stretched to the splitting point. If this woman really is Cristina, I remember that she's my friend. Cristina has a stronger claim to that title than Marie-Gabrielle or Alison, who are, as best I can recall, nothing more than cheerful companions, in whom one would never think of confiding, because any admission of weakness, of any tiny private anxiety, would be met with frosty disapproval and nothing more. Have I ever revealed anything at all to Cristina? Certainly not, it's not in my nature. But her entire person is awash with sympathy, with understanding just waiting to be called on. I then thought, in a surge of abandon, that the woman in green beside her banana tree might have been waiting for just that: for me to unburden my heart to her.

"Oh, this has never happened to me before," says Cristina in her hoarse, muffled voice. "There are two things, and they're both different from each other . . . The first . . . you already know . . . I, you know, I left the kids . . . for two days, I think . . . two or three days . . . with my parents, yes, for a holiday . . . just a little holiday . . . at grandma and grandpa's . . . and . . . you know my kids, you know them . . . are they . . . how can I put this . . . are they intolerable . . . coarse . . . completely disobedient?"

"Not at all," I say, taken aback.

As I remember, my friend Cristina has no children. In which case, who is this woman?

"No one could say that . . . call my kids that," she goes on. "Oh, they like to run around . . . they . . . they're full of energy . . . like all children . . . children today . . . vigorous, healthy. . . . Anyway, they're out at grandma and grandpa's . . . at my parents', I mean, and yesterday, Sunday, I go . . . you understand . . . I go . . . get them . . . pick them up, and I drive up to the house . . . grandma and grandpa's house . . . my parents' house . . . and it was . . . oh, absolutely silent . . . just . . . just the insects cheeping . . . maybe . . . absolutely silent . . . and I tell myself . . . they're . . . they're all taking a nap. I don't want to bother them . . . so . . . I don't jiggle the bell . . . the big metal bell on the gate . . . so I . . . I climb over the hedge . . . a hole . . . a sort of hole, a low spot . . . in the hedge . . . and I climb over it, without making a sound . . . and I come to . . . the terrace . . . and there . . . I hear . . . my God, I hear . . . someone crying . . . a man crying and I . . . I look . . . I look through the glass door and I see . . . I see my father, grandpa . . . papa, quietly crying . . . in front of grandma, my mother . . . she's standing there, helpless . . . her arms hanging limp . . . head down . . . pitiful, miserable . . . oh, that's the first time . . . my father crying . . . first time I've seen him . . . anyway . . . and he's talking . . . no, he's almost shouting . . . and my God, he says . . . he says . . . and he's talking about my kids, I can tell . . . his grandchildren . . . who really aren't all that . . . right?. . . About my kids on holiday with them . . . he says . . . to my mother . . . 'I can't take them anymore, I can't take them anymore' . . . and he also . . . also says . . . 'I'm leaving, I can't stay here, I can't stay in this house with them here' . . . and he's talking, you understand, about my . . . about my kids . . . and I . . . I left . . . discreetly . . . I climbed over the hedge the other way and then . . . I . . . I came back . . . later . . . and everything was ... everything seemed

. . . normal . . . just two kids on holiday at grandma and grandpa's . . . and I knew . . . I knew . . . that wasn't how it was . . . wasn't how it really was at all!"

Two tears rolled out from under Cristina's (?) tinted lenses. I wasn't sure what to say. What bond was there between us? And was she not guilty of having such children? Who was she? I really couldn't think what to say. I was looking down at Cristina's thick brown sandals. I took the little bits of lilac leaves from my pocket and carefully crumbled them over her feet.

"The other thing," says Cristina, "maybe you've already heard . . ."

No, I answer playfully, I never hear anything. And since, for anyone who knows me, that's an obvious, barefaced lie, I tell myself that if this woman really is my friend Cristina she'll protest, give me a little swat on the shoulder—but no, she goes on, grim-faced, standing perfectly still.

"A bunch of us saw it, in our yards, on the riverbank, in . . . Apparently there were even people who saw it in the schoolyard. The mayor . . . the mayor knows all about it. He saw it too. Something black, and quick. Oh, there were plenty of people who saw it."

Cristina's words are coming faster now. Her voice is sharper than usual. With a little hop she pulls her legs together and keeps them that way, squeezed tight. I ask:

"What is it? What did it turn out to be?" "You haven't seen anything?" Cristina asks. "

But what is it?"

"You haven't seen anything?"

All at once she pulls off her sunglasses. And then it's clear, I don't know that face. On the opposite sidewalk a young woman waves in my direction. It's Cristina, wearing little pink shorts.

"You haven't seen anything?" the first woman says again, and her tone is at once urgent, suspicious, and frightened.

I resolve not to keep this conversation up one moment longer. She vigorously wriggles her right foot, without looking at it or lowering her eyes, to shake off the shredded lilac leaves. Then she shoots me a glance full of unspoken anguish, whirls around, and hurries off, raising little clouds of dust under her sandals.

I'm so rattled I hardly notice Cristina crossing the street in her tiny pink shorts, with her graceful, jaunty gait. She kisses me twice on each cheek and I inhale her flowery scent. Cristina smells like a spring flower, a simple white flower. What she then says I'm not sure I can believe myself. Still, I know I didn't imagine it. She really does say it, however unlikely it seems. In a whisper, she says to me:

"A bunch of us saw it, in our yards, on the river- bank, in . . . Apparently there were even people who saw it in the schoolyard. The mayor . . . the mayor knows all about it. He saw it too. Something black, and quick. Oh, there were plenty of people who saw it."

What could I have answered, if not:

"But what is it?"

Cristina shrugs, vaguely spreading her arms. Her chin tenses, quivers. Cristina is usually such an impetuous woman that at first I don't grasp the depth of her distress.

"No one knows," she murmurs.

Cristina is very pretty. Little girls turn and stare when she walks by. I'm proud to have such a charming, vivacious woman as my friend, a woman who can wear a pair of tiny pink shorts with credibility and good humor. I'm grateful to her, because now I recognize her so perfectly. I put one arm around her shoulder to reassure her, I'm not sure about what. Her shoulders sag. She's completely disarmed. Seeing that, I don't press her to tell me anything more.

"The town's sent some workers to go search the school grounds," Cristina continues. "I'm on my way there myself. I'm worried."

Why so worried, I ask myself, since she doesn't have any children? And consequently, I ask myself: did I recognize her as perfectly as I thought?

Once the schoolyard and the little adjoining woods have been fruitlessly searched, I get back in my car and head for our house, a few kilometers from town. It's already near noon. Three hours have gone by since I set off for the school, and I never noticed. Could it be that the woman in green shorts, that stranger I took for Cristina, who must herself have confused me with someone she knew, could that woman really have kept me there talking for two full hours? It doesn't seem likely. Also, I think about that scene she described for me, the weeping father revealing his hatred for his grandchildren, and it seems naggingly close to something I've heard or read before. Either someone once told me about it or it comes from a novel that woman and I both happen to have read. And then she acted it out, while I listened—and I wonder: was I acting too? And did she realize I wasn't? But was she acting herself ? There, then, are all the things I don't know. Now I'm in a hurry to get home so I can look through my books and find the one where she might have found that story. For that matter, I could well be mistaken, and that scene is reminding me of another, almost identical, and in that case fictional, while the first is simply drawn from the false Cristina's existence.

I know I can't go straight home, and that makes me a little impatient, or maybe apprehensive. It's noon, and the sun is beating down starkly on the water-willow fields. This hot day has left us all a little downhearted, I think, anticipating the summer that's still to come, exhausted in advance.

I park in front of the house with the banana tree. The woman in green is gone now. A shiver of relief, almost triumph, quickly mutes my surprise and disappointment. I tell myself: my children had it exactly right, there never was a . . .

I get out of the car all the same. I push open the gate and start down the walk. I look up toward the second-floor balcony. The sunlight is dazzling. I shade my eyes with one hand, and that's when I see her, up on the balcony. Then she straddles the railing and throws herself off. I'm very aware of my little smile. Because I'm saying to myself: is all this really real?

A little later I'm sitting in the kitchen of that house I so often passed by, never dreaming I might one day go inside.

Litoral Array

Mahwash Shoaib

convex
portrait
mirrors
chartreuse
choral
rumi
capital
clocks
polymer
koyal
fen
clearly
collared
equates
cleaving
wracks

the
callow
hert
clubs
hope
lest
hacks
closest
lingus
clusters
éclair
licking
squealer
klimt's
aquiline
crest

cave
scrim
web
hibernus
yaar
scales
crag
shadow
drops
quake
clamp
celan
cliff
cloistered
crystal
zone

bar
none
level
copper
figged
slide
wet
copse
law
clammy
limbo
milk
kyun?
dance
collateral
release

Too Solid Flesh

for Anu Lakhan

Vahni Capildeo

Cross the road and you can walk south into an urban space that looks immemorial. Aston's Eyot is the site of a nineteenth-century midden; an old dump. The refuse heated up underground. Apple cores and pear seeds and walnut kernels matured into a wilderness too hybridized for names. Sprays of blackberries and rosehips arch red and black; sloes add notes of steely blue; a willow grows askant a brook. Other walkers are seldom met or heard. There are trodden paths but also many turnings.

She four-thousand-miles-away-across-the-ocean hasn't been herself lately. She hermits more and more. She would have liked the walk. Now I am home for another Saturday night…

"My thoughts have turned to green leaves."

"Well, that's better than sorrow. I'm so tired of living in this nameless sadness, even I am bored by myself."

"Do you keep a diary? A document of marvellous and total self-obsession?"

She feels like an invalid of centuries past, to be rolled out into the sun.

Who would push the chair? A lithe and grateful illiterate youth?

"A brilliant lavender and lace parasol-carrying creature with an air of reckless innocence..."

She four-thousand-miles-away-across-the-ocean has often felt, as have many others, that she is disconnected from her corporeal self. I am feeling out of touch with my body: it feels like something I have been given to look after. When I bathe I feel that I am washing it, not that I am bathing. She likes that I speak of it as being a thing I take care of, like a costume or a small animal.

How do I take care of it? Why is it not mine? Might a description get me closer to making it mine, or at least an understanding of why I am at odds with it?

She-who-hermits-more-and-more offers a description: leaning over a claw-footed tub, body costume in hand, I may gently soap and groom it... bathe it in milk and rose petals...take delicate brushes to it... do I? For it needs to understand not what it doesn't have but what it needs.

She desires me to immerse myself in the hows and whys.

The howls and wiles!

It wants things.

It is an idiot child.

It understandeth not that there is no store of warmth.

It has forgotten thirst.

A reminder to myself: water, at least every three hours. A reminder from myself: nudity, between clothing it at least twice a day. A reminder of myself: carefulness, up and down the steep expressionist stairs.

It wakes expectant. The look of ceiling meets its eye, or the look of curtain. Expectancy is worst.

A reminder, not to expect?

No. Clinging helplessly to its capabilities, ever hopeful of change, it issues reminders that are first cousin to cravings.

For her, in the sun perhaps; certainly elsewhere; like me, insufficiently solid; for her, this description, a near-total avoidance of the one with which I was tasked.

Because I am superstitious, I am stringing a series of lights between this and anything else that happens.

***

It was inconceivable to me that there had been nothing on the land in the residential area of Port of Spain where my family's house was built, though I knew the construction date was in 1971, and some of the building materials from the quarry my grandfather owned; thereby his ill elder son and unarranged daughter-in-law were enabled to hide respectably and save face for the family. There is no such thing as nothing.

Our storybooks were English and children in them ran around thousand-year-old castles or two-hundred-year-old vicarages; our myths were Hindu and we were encouraged to imagine many civilizations in a universe cyclically created and destroyed; and our island geography, we were told, had been Arawak and Carib.

The land sloped down, just over a quarter of an acre of it. There were mostly well-behaved trees and one frightening one, but there was also somehow the feeling of where trees had been. I do not mean stumps or even irregularities in the ground. There was more to this than the suggestion of seeding patterns of kush grass and razor grass, windflowers, lily spathes and snake plants. A child not allowed, for all sorts of reasons, to play much with other children started to know the nameless lilac trumpets, no bigger than two millimetres, that never did figure in textbooks; the partly concreted-over gap into unfathomable dark, possibly created by earthquake or earlier watercourses, which the grown-ups placed stones in front of only to find the stones moved away just enough to let something muscular through; and the patches of brooding that you might explain by the humidity of a present microclimate, but which I took to be the past knotting up of fibres into the concentration of a tree.

It was indoors, just inside the threshold of my bedroom, that I dreamt the woman who had tan yellow skin and a shearing rag of silk for hair. She was not the unwrapped mummy from the dead-house museums abroad. She was not quite my aunt's maid, who was over here from South America and was the first 'Arawak' I thought I had ever seen, since we were mis-taught that ours were extinct from ancient conflicts. She was more like that, though; yes, indigenous, a category scarcely acknowledged in Trinidad, to which people have been waves. She smiled at me and her smile went up toothily at the corners, because her flesh no longer covered skull.

"I'm as solid as you are," she said loudly and tonguelessly. Her arms extended themselves and my upper arms were grasped hard between the elbow and shoulder. "I'm as solid as you are."

I knew she could not be.

"I'm solid as you are."

But I was alive, and she was not. I broke free and woke up. I arrayed my mind with ferocity and identified a day.

***

It should be early evening. Can you see the individual flames, and the bronze tiger?

Janaki is tall. When she opened the wardrobe and I saw the array of clothes, it seemed right. There is stateliness in her modesty. The formal garments glistering there matched her presence almost weight for weight. She is pure gold.

A statue, moving: does that call up a nightmare scene? Why? A statue, moving: can that instil a sense of peace? It is, is so. Each gesture it makes should be made with consideration: otherwise it risks breaking itself or crushing that which it would reach or touch. Respecting its own range of possible movements, it would respect your space. If it made an approach, it could never be appropriate. It could only approximate you, so wearily, as only stone can be weary, for its way of breathing is to lose itself: each micropore exhales dust in a tiny brightening of the air, and with each exhalation the stone is less.

I read today of the man in his early forties pierced to death by metal as he dismantled a bridge under government orders.

There are inevitabilities that need not have become inevitable had there been the difference made by thought.

A statue, moving: pure matter so considered as to have identity with pure thought? Pure is a strange word.

Anyway, it took both hands for me to lift one of those garments on its wooden hanger. I imagined her inhabiting it, thin-backed, barefoot and gracious in mud or on tiles in that territory where a dream of the village East washes through into somewhere western, momentarily eroding the reality of both, sometimes leaving permanent alterations in its wake; somewhere like Trinidad, so Indian even if not considered so, so Western even if not called so, thumbnail of the Americas, immigrant blood opal at its base.

The weight of it I couldn't bear though I loved her for wanting to lend it to me. I gave up. I was the ghost.

The need to acquire weight followed me north and overseas. Imagine a pointilliste vision given an order of dismissal: the dots of colour that vibrate until the eye interlinks them and learns the trick of making sense of the person or the landscape depicted, these dots would obediently dance apart, disperse, making image into worse than nonsense, hurting the eye that tries to focus into questing after a scattering in which each particle is adamantine uncollectable. Being looked at, I was that unmade image, that hurt in return.

People who talked to me were unable to keep their countenance. I was not as dense as the object would need to be for them to focus on it. Their question, "Where is she from?" in my very presence became, "Where is she?"

I had the unfortunate effect of making segments of their heads disappear. These did not always reappear positioned correctly. This effect was deathlike in that nobody was immune. So you will better understand that, I shall tell you about the Armed Forces man. He had the kindness to ignore the others at the dinner table, in order to explain to me how I might acquire density: essentially, I was the same as any woman, if we could put aside the intellect. Abruptly, he took on the aspect of a pegged grapefruit of which one quarter had been eaten. His head not only disappeared; it also came apart.

The Armed Forces man's voice continued to make itself heard. Others around the table nodded vigorous support of his views. Now all of them were missing something. A solid and crystalline seam of absence scarred them from temple to jawbone. I searched in vain for any faces. Voices kept tilting out of voids. I got up and left the table in some distress.

I had not yet decided to abandon the scene, so I exited to the bathroom, where iridescent lights were strung across the bathtub and there was no shower and no soap. I looked in the mirror and did not see myself, which brought some comfort. A classic moment had enveloped me. The same had happened to Vidia Naipaul's father; but in his time, non-being brought with it horror and insult. I could and did wait. That I was a trick of the light, I accepted. Failing to pull myself together, I left the party without embarrassment, indeed without a proper farewell, and started walking.

The knife crime boys were not at the end of the road that day. At the corner I passed a woman pushing a pram. She was chatting to another woman, who carried a bag of shopping. They were not as old as I am. More had happened around their eyes. They seemed to see and not see me. Their aura of sociability expanded, spreading with a faint juddering as they drew near. They walked me off the pavement into the gutter.

I was too horrified to say "Excuse me". The hands in charge of the baby carriage had no wrists. A seam of void extended beyond the sleeves. No cross-section of bone and pulsing bluecrimson evidenced itself. Just solidity again, palpable absence. The same apparent chasm joined the set of fingers grasping the plastic shopping bag to the pinkish banister of arm. The women moved like a staircase next to a lift shaft down which I and my kind dropped.

Reading, a sedentary occupation except on places like the London train, where tickets are sold after the last seat is gone, and the area of corridor between First Class and standard class carriages is much coveted by those who can find floor early enough to settle down with a book until forced upright by the briefcased, backpacked, mobile telephone users... Reading could fix me. It could be a way to acquire weight. Consider the women in academic posts, whose faces are keener than normal and who rise like bells from an ever widening base. I have seen one such white-stockinged and long-skirted in the south-west, and dared not wonder how long it would take for her legs to meld together into one. Then she would ring out and trundle towards the apex of a career, wild for the literature that has been written, for no more need be written, for literature is the province of the dead, and how can I have something to add to it? To the bells that clamour over the greening inscriptions, I can but ghost the living past...

I opened a book and a mango fell out. I opened another, and another mango fell out. These were newly published books: fresh leaves.

Woman doth not live by mango alone. Was there more goodness in volumes of essays or in novels? Were specialist shops and second-hand departments a good bet in the search for sustenance?

After a couple of weeks or perhaps ten or twelve years, with something like desperation I totalled the yield, excluding mangos:

2 quarts desiccated coconut

1 breadfruit

Half a yam

A grain of salt

A grain of match

A piece of camphor

1 measure sweet (maraschino)

10 measures sour (lime)

100 measures strong (rum)

1 tin condensed milk (for sandwiches)

1 tin condensed milk (for tea)

5 enamel cups

Cream crackers

Curried shrimp

A 1950s bookmark with a school crest defaced with the motto *Sufficient unto the dhal is the weevil thereof* (fountain pen, italic)

(I did not buy the book that had the tablecloth)

(The coal pot presumably had been removed by the police after he was found to have succumbed to carbon monoxide poisoning)

This left over a hundred and seventy mangos, despite the careful selection process.

"I do not know what to do with all these mangos."

"Take them to market," said the agent with half a face.

"The same ones?"

"You were glad enough to find them, weren't you?" he said, answerably.

Mine is one of the few corners of the city not assailed by pigeons. On my way to buy the weightiest bread I could, I noticed the absence of pigeons; for the food of many peoples was strewn or for sale along the pavements. A lot of reading must have been going on, if even a few of these nostalgic, often faintly toxic fruits had fallen from the leaves of books. A volatile, ratty iridescence of pigeons would have flocked towards such riches in Oxford city centre, but there are seldom such spills between the spires; perhaps nobody reads there at all, or perhaps the opening of books is no such unsealing.

A woman friend with a head full of music and hips like a cello… solider than I am…once met me in the market square among those urbo-centric pigeons, her face phosphorescent with fear. That was when I began finding out how widespread pigeon phobia is, in the south of England; as inconvenient in its way as the well-diagnosed lizard phobia in the Caribbean.

How different the child with bronze fluff for hair who had laughed in the streets of Florence as he went towards the pigeons and stamped. Again and again he stamped, his face a forum for the mingling of cruelty and glee. The birds, stupid with alarm, went and settled, went and settled, not seeming to identify an attacker, unable to deal with the repeated fact that they could not stay in what they felt to be their place. He was an infant Perseus. He was cause; the rest of the world, effect. He impressed me as much as that other Perseus, bronze all through and smiling slenderly but solidly in the Piazza, the head of the Medusa in his hand.

Medusa's beautiful, wise serpentine head was cut off because she paralyzed people who looked at her. Was that it, or did people fear being seen through by her? Could they not bear to be known? Not by her, not as she could know. Crying paralysis, they stopped themselves in the presence of an amoral scrutiny in which everything is as it is, not as anyone would have it be, and the intricate is simple. Medusa's head was co-opted as a weapon, to be brought out of the man's bag when enemies needed to be stopped. Was this change of use good or bad or neither?

One thing for sure: her quality of living contemplation had ceased to be in the possession of a female form moving with the constancy of the living. It had been made deathly, after being marked for death.

Bronze was ringing and serpents twirling somewhere in the past's past as I turned the corner.

I was solider than the girl behind the counter of the shop. She had a saline pallor like a washed rind cheese. The shelves were clean, but darkness clustered like flies; not darkness that one could see…it made the space between the wrappers of untranslated *s/z* sweets heavy with something yet more adaptable than shadow. The bread there was cheap and good, and I needed to acquire weight. If I met her eyes during our transaction, she too might solidify some more. This would benefit the neighbourhood. A slice of air circulating among the merchandise was clearly another customer who had disappeared altogether on seeing me in the wrong pigeonhole. (This shop was without salt fish or mangos.) The loaf, chock full of seeds, was the right size for a one-person household.

I took pleasure in the quietening of the street. A laugh, here and there, closed a shutter of air on the temporary private room of a pavement hello or goodbye. Light thickened. The small, dense grains opened strange flavours to the inside of my mouth. Changes were occurring in what my mind could visually process. Twilight was general throughout my apartment. A plain spread wide in my imagination. The scene constructed itself as I saw less and less of my actual surroundings. Terror and relief came at the moment of realization. Greyish green and dark brown, the almost-black of a cold field, and hair tossing in the abandonment of earth; pale limbs, shaped and furred similar to those I had known; and recent roots, shallow, hard at work, drawing out of the soil their nourishment from the uncountable breaking down of human beings into scandalously lamentable flesh. I saw the sprouting and greening of the plain, and the sheaves ripening towards harvest. The bread that was to have made me solid had undone itself and nearly undone me. I finished the meal. I could not finish the loaf. It was a hungry thing. There was too much time in it.

The glass overcoat was manufactured, if not developed, in that country where the grains of the loaf had grown. The glass overcoat gave automatic density. It was cast in one, seamless, except for tiny bubbling within the glass, like you get in marbles. Scratch-resistant and shatterproof, it was admittedly chill; less so to the wearer, who felt insulated by the build-up of body heat; felt, if anything, more flexible, within the range of movement that did remain possible. The people in glass overcoats spent a lot of time in transit. The main drawbacks to contact with others were evident. The smudges from everyday wear translated to rainbows. These were not so much a problem as was the gritty rain of that climate. This style of garment is out of fashion and no longer exported. Dubiously collectable, some turn up second-hand in England. Buying one and wearing it would show a real investment in…something.

The loneliness of the body is utterly different from the loneliness of the mind. Ready to race ahead, the mind is impatient when the body, untouched by anyone day after day, begins to shiver as bedtime draws near. The hands catch and hurt when undoing a button. They refuse to deal with the edge of the book, which tumbles to the floor, leaves flying. This shiver is not a thing of the surface. It is a shuddering from within, as if cold breaks out on the skin from a heart splintered into a rose of frost. Then the weightlessness of the bed must be resisted. It wants to assume the body. A wind of separateness drives at the outline of each fold and bend battered by ice. Sleep will not take under these conditions. A summer that dries out the linens within hours has no effect on the ague of isolation. A layer of black wool has to be worn at night-time in the hottest month of the year. The being practised in isolation not reconciling itself to the exercise in cruelty that is dream... It wakes warm and looks about, the body ready for a round of greetings. The mind knowing otherwise, ordering the smile wiped off the face, the tender weakness in the fingers to tense up, wakes a little annoyed at the insistence with which it is tipped into disappointment, having nothing to do but begin in silence and space, meeting only its own demands, without refreshment from a contradictory presence.

The scission, when I finished losing my body, was in January. Christmas was just past and I was due to travel up to Scotland for Hogmanay, so it was still the Old Year, the turn of winter over the calendar, when the high fever set in. I was invited to come north anyway, and be looked after; but I was not strong enough to deposit my temperature on the train and carry my germs across the Border.

I had been aware of greater tiredness than normal, but what is normal? Winter in Oxford was a scant pause for the trees that minded their own business and continued more or less strenuously to branch and bud. A layer of coconut frosting on the ground looked more like a birthday cake than serious weather, and disappeared faster.

So, this winter was not normal. The tall nineteenth-century windows that let in light from the south and west were filled with blackness in between falling snow. The snow fell, and settled, and went on falling. The snow settled, and did not melt, and more snow fell. A small white dog could have been buried in the amounts that drifted up around the annexe door. Twigs were coated to several times their thickness. The roofs of the next door pub and its add-on buildings could have been any shape under their pitiless cover. At whatever hour that I looked out, there were the lines and monuments of this winter's victory; and those were many hours.

For my tiredness was not normal. Overnight the skin of my face blistered and began to peel off like paint on a badly neglected wall. I had no thermometer. Was this fever? Morning after morning my lips, stuck together with dryness, needed lotion rubbed into them before they would open and I could drink water. They cracked deeply and widely at the corners, visible slits as if made by a letter-opener, and bled as I took the first sips. I dabbed with a tissue, and saw scarlet. The cracks blistered but would not fill up with flesh or cover over with scab. The reasons I did not immediately ring the doctor are not to be told here; suffice it to say that I was too accustomed to people who varied between unseeing and unseen.

I creamed my lips and watched the winter. I became frightened only when the lead box installed itself in my rib cage: walking from the bedroom to the kitchen necessitated a stop on the sofa, and lifting a glass brought on hyperventilation.

Let these procedures not be questioned.

I visited the official website. The website diagnosed me with official swine flu. No tests would be done. I took the number I was issued, and knew it was pointless to call my doctor, for I could not get myself to that location. The official website informed me that everyone ill in Britain needed a 'flu friend', who would collect their medication. I rang a few acquaintances who might have stayed at home during the festive season. Their mobiles connected to differently pitched signals: international ones: before switching to answerphone. The woman in the flat above me had gone away. As usual, footsteps or creaky boards sounded in her empty flat; they were of no use. No post was being delivered through the snow, so there was no point looking for a pileup on the stairs that might tell me nobody had been in at all. I listened out. The great emptiness assured me that this house, divided into flats, was holding itself in during the snow. I was its breathing.

The official website directed me to the so-called Primary Care Trust.

Relieved to see they were located in my neighbourhood, I rang. Soon antibiotics would drop through the brass flap; I would wander germily down the stairs, making rest stops when the lead box was awkward, and wander back up to start waging internal war against the infection. The person who answered the phone had an audible conversation with his colleague. *If she doesn't have a number and she hasn't spoken to her GP we don't have to give her the Tamiflu.* I gave the number several times, to two people, in the course of a few minutes. Each time, they seemed not to remember that I had consulted the website and given them an official number. I pushed back memories of Passport Control, and the memorable twenty minutes when I reiterated where I live or where I was born and the blandness of my desired voyaging…the classical music of the wrong origin; twenty minutes is long enough to perform some concertos. The Primary Care Trust would call me back.

The woman on the other end of the phone raised her voice and began a patter like a fishmonger desperate to move on her rotting wares and raise enough money to cover her husband's rum habit. *I had to have family; friends; co-workers; neighbours…?* You seem to have difficulty in understanding that someone might be alone at Christmas. *There must be someone…!* Only a friend, one of those truly dear friends who nonetheless are seen fewer than five times a year, in another village, expecting a second child, living with her toddler…exactly the Flu Friend to brave the House of Plague… *Well, if she's pregnant the child can't be* that *small!…* I realized that she had elicited a biography from me: of immigration, a broken relationship and unemployment: an analysis of how doors close on English houses during their holidays. The lead box was pressing closer to the surface of my chest. I raised my voice in turn and dehumanized the woman and rang off, and fell asleep with the effort of it. I woke to the doorbell. The reluctant health worker walked up a couple of stairs and extended her arm like a kindergarten flag waver at a national parade. I smiled infectiously at her and started down the stairs. With undisguised horror she thrust the tiny packet in its oversized envelope towards me, and fled.

Let these procedures not be questioned.

By this time I was not solid at all. I had the colours of Snow White: lips as red as blood (but in the wrong way); sky and hair black as ebony; and the slant of descending white to look at. What was inside, what was outside? I stopped trying to contact anyone, and found it would be two weeks or more before anyone would contact the childless, no-news nowherian. In those days something changed.

This was the first spring of disconnection.

*So why not you and I…*a music-box dusting itself off as its ballerina figurine twirls… Some melody played itself in previous springs, as pollen blew and temperate colours reasserted themselves waxily, waterishly, pink and white; the external and internal flickered up again, *always*….

This year I knew that had been youth. Spring would not come again with a sense of oneness. It was not in my future to soften and burgeon. The young kangaroo mothers and grim boyish lovers and ice-cream-on-a-stick screaming mess of children, the leafmeal and paper-wrapper litter swirled together, adhered to railings and bus stop signs, washed up again and toppled and proceeded to paint the city with an impression of life.

The hearts of the roses outside the Botanic Garden were an embarrassment of potential. The depth, the disclosure… Out of rhythm with the natural process, I became gentler with old people and thought about soldiers, whether for them spring had elements of homecoming.

The sun is so bright, the eye is a blackboard. The car approaching the crossroads slows down. Four walls of shimmering air are too much for the mind's eye. It perceives and makes memories of what it sees as if sitting in a cool classroom. A woman in white is waiting to cross the

East Oxford road. She flutters. Her silhouette, instantly recognizable, feels extra familiar; her clothing is old-fashioned North Indian.

So much of cloth. An older woman's voice whispers disapproval in my ear. Why so much of cloth, when dresses would not be frowned on by the guardians of good behaviour? My grandmother's generation was already permitted to wear colonial-export challis cotton or georgette print, fastened with covered buttons like those on living room furniture. The knees would not quite be exposed. The uncovered legs might be sturdy, twentieth-century varicose originals of the limbs adored in bronze or sandstone by pre-Christian-era sculptors. The uncovered legs might be spindly, kin to those that bend again and again among the leaves of some labour-intensive crop on its way towards the airtight hold of a fragrant destiny. The partly razored legs might be sleek with cocoa butter or coconut oil, rubbed in by the hands of grandchildren who learn the mysteries of pain and age from the question-command, "Come and rub your Ajee's legs!"

If you see the pictures like Auntie Sati had — you remember the batik pictures? — we never covered ourselves up. Covering ourselves up, that is a new thing. Maybe it is a Muslim thing, maybe it is a Western thing. Those women in the pictures, some of them are not even wearing a choli. They tie their sari across their bare chest. I do not know whether what the older voice says is true.

Widow: the white drapery identifies the woman poised at the kerbside. White-is-the-colour-of-brides-black-is-the-colour-of-mourning: no. Dissonant and spectral associations have to be pushed away when I sit in a church whose stony atmosphere is fertilized by the overspilling of satin and orchids and tears of joy as the bride navigates the aisle. The strong florals are overlaid by those of a tropical night and the cool striking up under my feet seems to strike up more directly. Sitting in church in the afternoon, facing a crucifix, I am standing barefoot in a marble courtyard in the dark, the Dancing Shiva at my back, the Kali shrine still to be built. A row of women assembles itself on foldup metal chairs. They are in white drapery and look so much alike, whited out in widowhood, that I embrace my great-aunt, taking her for my grandmother.

Because I am superstitious, I am stringing a series of lights here once more.

***

"Black," my mother says darkly, "is a colour of joy." Kali is black. Black contains all the colours; it is ultimate colour.

Can you see the flame in front of the bronze tiger?

The wick has blackened and at the base of the flame is a note of steely blue. Reflections shine red-gold.

Yesterday I walked again in the green space.

This has been thought for you.

Contributors

Vahni Capildeo was born in Trinidad. She went to Britain in 1991, and completed a DPhil in Old Norse at Oxford in 2000. Her poetry includes *No Traveller Returns* (2003), *Person Animal Figure* (2005), and *Undraining Sea* (2009).

Amy Sara Carroll, assistant Professor of American Culture, Latina/o Studies, and English at the University of Michigan, Ann Arbor, is the author of two collections of poetry *SECESSION* (Hyperbole Books, 2012) and *FANNIE + FREDDIE/The Sentimentality of Post⊠9/11 Pornography* (Fordham University Press, 2013). Since 2008, she also has been a member of Electronic Disturbance Theater 2.0/b.a.n.g. lab, coproducing the *Transborder Immigrant Tool.* Currently, Carroll is completing her first critical monograph "REMEX: Toward an Art History of the NAFTA Era,"under contract with the University of Texas Press.

Saudamini Deo is a writer and photographer from India.

Writer and filmmaker **Dia Felix** is author of the Lambda-nominated experimental novel "Nochita," published on City Lights/Sister Spit in 2014. Areas of interest include romance, celebrity, obsession, decadence, modernity, and rock and roll. She's screened films and read at very many places including Segue, Radar Reading Series, The New Museum, and Albertine Books. She's published recently with Ping Pong, a journal of the Henry Miller Library, The Feminist Wire, and Poetry Project Newsletter. She curates a pan-genre literary performance series, GUTS, at Dixon Place and founded and heads the maybe-fictional enterprise Personality Press. She's from California and lives in East Harlem, New York.

Marlin M. Jenkins is learning how to love himself. Born and raised in Detroit, he is a poetry student in University of Michigan's MFA program. His writings have been given homes by The Collagist, The Journal, Word Riot, and The Offing, among others. You can find him online at marlinmjenkins.tumblr.com and @Marlin_Poet.

Angela Karee: Born & raised on Chicago's south side (Englewood!). Currently struggling to successfully raise a garden, two children and a bulldog with the love of her life in the quiet of the burbs.

Magda Kapa, born in Greece and now living in northern Germany, worked as a freelance screenwriter and Modern Greek and English teacher. Her first poetry collection All the Words was published by Phoenicia Publishing. She is also a photographer and blogs http://notborninenglish.wordpress.com/ and tweets as @MagdaKapa.

Kim Dana Kupperman is the author of the essay collection, *I Just Lately Started Buying Wings: Missives from the Other Side of Silence*, and, forthcoming in November 2016, *The Last of Her: A Forensic Memoir*. She is the founding editor of Welcome Table Press, a nonprofit independent press devoted to publishing and celebrating the essay. She is a guest faculty member at West Virginia Wesleyan's low-residency MFA Program and teaches in Johns Hopkins University's MA in Writing Program.

Karen An-hwei Lee is the author of *Phyla of Joy* (Tupelo 2012), *Ardor* (Tupelo 2008) and *In Medias Res* (Sarabande 2004), winner of the Norma Farber First Book Award. Lee also wrote two chapbooks, *God's One Hundred Promises* (Swan Scythe 2002) and *What the Sea Earns for a Living* (Quaci Press 2014). Her book of literary criticism, *Anglophone Literatures in the Asian Diaspora: Literary Transnationalism and Translingual Migrations* (Cambria 2013), was selected for the Cambria Sinophone World Series. She earned an M.F.A. from Brown University and Ph.D. in English from the University of California, Berkeley. The recipient of a National Endowment for the Arts Grant, Lee is a voting member of the National Book Critics Circle. Currently, she lives in San Diego and serves in the university administration at Point Loma Nazarene University.

Aurora Masum-Javed is a poet, performer, and educator. She is currently completing her MFA in poetry at Cornell. Her work has been published or is forthcoming in *Jaggery*, *So to Speak*, and *Callaloo*. She was recently a fellow at the Squaw Valley Writers Workshop and the Callaloo Creative Writing Workshop.

Miranda Mellis is the author of *Demystifications* (forthcoming, Solid Objects 2017); *The Instead*, a book-length dialogue with Emily Abendroth (Carville Annex 2016); *The Quarry* (Trafficker Press, 2013); *The Spokes* (Solid Objects, 2012); *None of This Is Real* (Sidebrow Press, 2012); *Materialisms* (Portable Press at Yo-Yo Labs, 2009); and *The Revisionist* (Calamari Press, 2007). Her stories and essays have appeared in various publications including *Harper's*, *The Believer*, *Conjunctions*, the *New York Times*, *Fence*, *McSweeney's* and elsewhere. She is an editor at *The Encyclopedia Project* and teaches at The Evergreen State College. Raised in the city of San Francisco, she now lives in the woods of the Pacific Northwest.

Saretta Morgan is Brooklyn-based reader/animal keeper/letter writer/ plant waterer and water color enthusiast interested in organization, [queer/public/adverse] intimacies, shame and being Black.

Leila Nadir is a writer and artist whose work focuses on environmental and food issues, evolutions of memory, and questions of ethnicity, identity, and belonging. She has a PhD in literature from Columbia University and is a former Mellon Foundation Environmental Humanities Post-Doctoral Fellow. Her essays and criticism have appeared in *North American Review*, *Asian American Literary Review*, *American Scientist*, *Leonardo*, and *Hyperallergic,* among other places. She is currently Lecturer in Sustainability and Environmental Humanities at the University of Rochester and is at work on a memoir, titled Cold War, about the colorful marriage of her Afghan, Muslim father and Slovak, Catholic mother, who together raised seven children.

Marie NDiaye is a French novelist and playwright. She published her first novel, *Quant au riche avenir*, when she was 17. She won the Prix Goncourt in 2009. Her play *Papa doit manger* is the sole play by a living female writer to be part of the repertoire of the Comédie française.

Janeil Page's poetry has been published most recently in *Bridge Eight Literary Magazine*, *Bluffs Literary Magazine* and as part of a collaborative poetry collection through Gold Quoin Press. She is a poet in a small town in Illinois and holds an MFA from Bennington Writing Seminars.

Janelle Poe is a writer, Harlemite, City College MFA student, DJ & digger who loves uncovering hidden gems and connections, finding this approach widely applicable. A background in International Studies and life as a black woman in America and abroad, she writes about the inherent intersectionality of injustice. A VONA participant, she is ever grateful for the leaders, including Aster(ix), crafting space for the expression and amplification of marginalized voices. Currently at work on a collection of short stories and essays, illustrious publications and titles are forthcoming. This is one. Following her dreams, she encourages you to follow yours. www.Elle-DJ.com.

Khadijah Queen is the author of *Conduit* (Akashic Books 2008), *Black Peculiar* (Noemi Press 2011), *Non-Sequitur* (Litmus Press 2015) and *Fearful Beloved* (Argos Books 2015). Her fifth book, *I'm So Fine: A List of Famous Men & What I Had On*, will be published in spring 2017 by YesYes Books. She teaches in the Mile-High MFA program at Regis University.

Laura Sims is the author of four books of poetry: *Staying Alive* (Ugly Duckling Presse, 2016), *My god is this a man*, *Stranger*, and *Practice, Restraint* (Fence Books). In 2014 she edited *Fare Forward: Letters from David Markson*, a book of her correspondence with the celebrated experimental novelist (powerHouse Books). Her work was included in The City Visible: Chicago Poetry for the New Century, and individual poems have recently appeared in *Black Clock*, *Black Warrior Review*, *Colorado Review*, *Denver Quarterly*, and*Gulf Coast*. She has published book reviews and essays in *Boston Review*, *Evening Will Come*, *Jacket*, *New England Review*, *Rain Taxi* and *The Review of Contemporary Fiction*.

Chika Unigwe is the author of three novels and several short stories. She is an Assistant Professor of Literary Arts at Brown University, Providence, RI. She is at work on a new novel and a short story collection

Sarah Vap is the author of six collections of poetry. Her most recent book, *Viability*, was selected by Mary Jo Bang for the National Poetry Series and was released by Penguin in 2016. She is the recipient of an NEA Literature fellowship for poetry and a Research Enhancement Fellowship from the University of Southern California for a year of writer and research in West Africa. She lives with her family in Venice, CA.

Acknowledgments

"Three Poems" by Khadijah Queen are from her forthcoming book *I'm So Fine: A List of Famous Men & What I Had On.*

Laura Sim's *Olga Poems* have previously appeared in The Opiate, Jerkpoet, and Touch the Donkey.

Amy Sara Carroll's untitled poem was first published in *Errata# Revista de Artes Visuales 3* (special issue on "Cultura Digital y Creación/Digital Culture and Creation" December 2010).

"St. George's Bell" by Magda Kapa appeared previously in *qarrtsiluni online literary magazine.*

"The Spokes (excerpt)" by Miranda Mellis was excerpted from T*he Spokes* published by Solid Objects in June 2012.

"Too Solid Flesh" by Vahni Capildeo, from *Measures of Expatriation* (2016), is copyrighted and is reprinted by kind permission of Carcanet Press Limited, Manchester, UK.

Marie NDiaye's piece, translated by Jordan Stump, is an excerpt from

Self-Portrait in Green (San Francisco: Two Lines Press, 2014). Printed with permission by Two Lines Press.

www.ingramcontent.com/pod-product-compliance
Lightning Source LLC
Chambersburg PA
CBHW032028180726
48284CB00008B/2517

9781942547044